The First-Year Experience® Monograph Series No. 52

INTERNATIONAL PERSPECTIVES
ON THE FIRST-YEAR EXPERIENCE IN HIGHER EDUCATION

Diane Nutt and Denis Calderon, Editors

**National Resource Center for
The First-Year Experience®
& Students in Transition**

UNIVERSITY OF SOUTH CAROLINA

In association with TEESSIDE UNIVERSITY

Cite as:

Nutt, D., & Calderon, D. (2009). International perspectives on the first-year experience in higher education (Monograph No. 52). Columbia, SC: University of South Carolina, National Resource Center for The First-Year Experience and Students in Transition.

Sample chapter citation:

O'Shea, S. (2008). Uni-Start: Student-led "Transition to Study" workshops. In D. Nutt & D. Calderon (Eds.), International perspectives on the first-year experience in higher education (Monograph No. 52, pp. 27-32). Columbia, SC: University of South Carolina, National Resource Center for The First-Year Experience and Students in Transition.

Copyright © 2009 University of South Carolina. All rights reserved. No part of this work may be reproduced or copied in any form, by any means, without written permission of the University of South Carolina.

ISBN 978-1-889-27166-8

The First-Year Experience® is a service mark of the University of South Carolina. A license may be granted upon written request to use the term "The First-Year Experience." This license is not transferable without written approval of the University of South Carolina.

Production Staff for the National Resource Center:

Project Manager	Tracy L. Skipper, Assistant Director for Publications
Project Editors	Barbara F. Tobolowsky, Associate Director; Trish Willingham, Editor; Toni Vakos, Editor; Emily Mullins and Dottie Weigel, Editorial Assistants
Design and Production	Erin Morris, Graphic Artist

Additional copies of this monograph may be obtained from the National Resource Center for The First-Year Experience and Students in Transition, University of South Carolina, 1728 College Street, Columbia, SC 29208. Telephone (803) 777-6229. Fax (803) 777-4699.

Library of Congress Cataloging-in-Publication Data

International perspectives on the first-year experience in higher education / Diane Nutt and Denis Calderon, editors.
    p. cm. -- (The first-year experience monograph series ; No. 52)
 Includes bibliographical references.
 ISBN 978-1-889271-66-8
 1. College freshmen--Cross-cultural studies. I. Nutt, Diane. II. Calderon, Denis. III. National Resource Center for the First-Year Experience & Students in Transition (University of South Carolina)
 LB2343.3.I59 2009
 378.1'98--dc22
                2009039647

Contents

Foreword 1
    Jennifer R. Keup & Tracy L. Skipper

The First-Year Experience: An International Perspective 3
    Diane Nutt & Denis Calderon

Overview of Countries 9
    Denis Calderon, Diane Nutt, & Associates

Australia

Uni-Start: Student-Led "Transition to Study" Workshops 27
    The University of Newcastle

Canada

Enhancing Performance: The Effectiveness of a Faculty
    of Fine Arts Peer Mentoring Program 33
    York University, Toronto

England

Retention Support Officers: Support for Students in Context 39
    Teesside University

Peer Assisted Study Sessions: Personalizing the Learning Experience 43
    The University of Manchester

Exploring the Use of E-portfolios and Blogs to Support the Transition Into
    Higher Education for Foundation Degree Students 49
    University of Wolverhampton

Japan

Developing Peer-Support Skills in Students 55
    Kansai University

Morocco

The First-Year Seminar 61
    Sidi Mohamed Ben Abdallah University

New Zealand

Holistic Intervention Program for At-risk Students 67
Auckland University of Technology

Peer-Assisted Transition and Induction for First-Time Entering Undergraduates 75
The University of Auckland

Northern Ireland

Enhancing Social Interaction Among Students and Staff Through the Use of
    Residential Events During Induction 81
University of Ulster

Portugal

Promoting First-Year Students' Learning Strategies Through Instructional Narratives 87
University of Minho

South Africa

The First-Year Academy: An Institution-Wide Initiative to Foster Student Success 95
Stellenbosch University

Sweden

The SciTech Model: From First Year to Career 101
Uppsala University

United States of America

Assessing Student Learning in Freshman Inquiry 109
Portland State University

The Efficacy of a Coordinated, Multilayered First-Year Experience Program 119
Purdue University

Wales

Faculty Advice Shops 125
University of Glamorgan

Conclusion 133
Diane Nutt & Denis Calderon

Glossary of Terms 137

About the Editors 139

Foreword

While our name—the National Resource Center for The First-Year Experience and Students in Transition—suggests that our work is grounded within a particular national context (i.e., the United States), we have long embraced a more global mission. In fact, the first International Conference on The First-Year Experience at Newcastle upon Tyne Polytechnic in England was held the year the Center was established in 1986. Since that time, we have sought to cultivate an international network of educators committed to the success of first-year students from diverse backgrounds who are entering a wide range of institutional types. In sponsoring this international network, we helped each other learn more about the experiences of entering college students within and across national boundaries; identified promising strategies for helping those students learn and succeed in postsecondary education institutions across the globe; and encouraged one another to engage in conversations about the design, implementation, and evaluation of those strategies.

The 22 International Conferences on The First-Year Experience have been the primarily vehicle for bringing this network together so that they can learn from one another. We have also encouraged regional dialogues on the first year of college, hosting the First Canadian-American Conference on The First-Year Experience in Toronto in 1988. We hosted four such meetings, and the conversations begun and ideas shared at those meetings are in part responsible for the monograph, *From Best Intentions to Best Practices: The First-Year Experience in Canadian Postsecondary Education*, which the Center published in 1997. In 1995, we assisted Queensland University of Technology in Australia in launching the Pacific Rim Conference on the First Year in Higher Education. More recently, we have been happy to lend support to the European Conference on the First Year Experience. Over time, we have begun to complement and continue this dialogue via international communication on the listservs sponsored by the National Resource Center, by hosting international scholars on visits to the Center, and through submissions from practitioners and researchers from other countries to our online newsletter, *E-Source for College Transitions*, and scholarly journal, *Journal on The First-Year Experience and Students in Transition*.

Regardless of the vehicle, when we discuss first-year issues across different national contexts, it often creates the perfect environment for us to reflect and revisit the basic tenets of our work with first-year students. It forces us to explain our terminology and articulate our assumptions. What do we mean when we use the terms *persistence, success, transition*, or even *first-year student* in our country and system of higher education? How are our experiences with first-year students different or similar when we look across countries, cultures, or social contexts? These are the types of rich conversations that provide an incredible opportunity for us to revisit what is familiar, learn about things that are different, connect in our similarities, and reconsider what is possible in our work with students. It is our hope that the content of this monograph will strengthen the foundation upon which to initiate or continue these conversations about the first-year experience movement on an international scale.

The format for this monograph is based on a highly successful series of volumes, *Exploring the Evidence*, that offers not only useful descriptions of programs but also research and assessment data, highlighting the effectiveness of these initiatives in helping first-year students achieve a wide range of learning outcomes and markers of college success. The *Exploring the Evidence* series initially focused only on research reports on first-year seminars in American higher education (Barefoot, 1993; Barefoot, Warnock, Dickinson, Richardson, & Roberts, 1998; Griffin & Romm, 2008;

Tobolowsky, Cox, & Wagner, 2005) but has recently expanded to include research-based descriptions of a wide range of first-year initiatives used in the United States (Troxel & Cutright, 2008), including peer mentor programs (Glisson, 2009). We are pleased to offer *International Perspectives on The First-Year Experience in Higher Education* as our latest collection of campus-based research reports and are excited to expand the scope of this series to an international focus. We hope that readers will find value in the descriptions of the wide range of initiatives for supporting first-year students, representing nearly a dozen counties and focusing on comprehensive programs, early-warning systems for at-risk students, the use of electronic portfolios, first-year seminars, learning communities, orientation or induction, peer mentoring, retention initiatives, self-regulated learning, and supplemental instruction or peer-assisted study sessions. We truly believe that learning from one another, sharing resources, and collaboration across institutions, systems, and countries will make all the difference as we go forward to face the challenges and seize the opportunities that lie ahead for higher education and the first-year experience.

We are extremely grateful to the editors, Diane Nutt and Denis Calderon, for identifying contributors for this volume and shepherding it to completion.

Jennifer R. Keup
Director

Tracy L. Skipper
Assistant Director for Publications

September 2009

References

Barefoot, B. O. (Ed.). (1993). *Exploring the evidence: Reporting outcomes of first-year seminars* (Monograph No. 11). Columbia, SC: University of South Carolina, National Resource Center for The Freshman Year Experience.

Barefoot, B. O., Warnock, C. L., Dickinson, M. P., Richardson, S. E., & Roberts, M. R. (Eds.). (1998). *Exploring the evidence: Reporting outcomes of first-year seminars, Volume II* (Monograph No. 25). Columbia, SC: University of South Carolina, National Resource Center for The First-Year Experience and Students in Transition.

Glisson, N. L. (Ed.). (2009). *Exploring the evidence: Reporting research on peer education programs* [online archive]. Columbia, SC: University of South Carolina, National Resource Center for The First-Year Experience and Students in Transition. Retrieved October 22, 2009, from http://sc.edu/fye/resources/fyr/peers.html

Griffin, A. M., & Romm, J. (Eds.). (2008). *Exploring the evidence: Reporting research on first-year seminars, Volume IV*. Columbia, SC: University of South Carolina, National Resource Center for The First-Year Experience and Students in Transition. Retrieved October 22, 2009, from http://www.sc.edu/fye/resources/fyr/index.html

Tobolowsky, B. F., Cox, B. E., & Wagner, M. T. (2005). *Exploring the evidence: Reporting research on first-year seminars, Volume III* (Monograph No. 42). Columbia, SC: University of South Carolina, National Resource Center for The First-Year Experience and Students in Transition.

Troxel, W. G., & Cutright, M. (2008). *Exploring the evidence: Initiatives in the first college year* (Monograph No. 49). Columbia, SC: University of South Carolina, National Resource Center for The First-Year Experience and Students in Transition.

The First-Year Experience: An International Perspective

Diane Nutt and Denis Calderon

This monograph is the result of collaborative efforts between the National Resource Center for The First-Year Experience and Students in Transition (NRC), Teesside University and the organizers of the European First Year Experience Conference series. Teesside University has been cohost for the National Resource Center's International Conferences on The First-Year Experience since 1988, and as such we have had an interest in the development of first-year initiatives beyond the USA.

Through its conferences, publications, and research efforts, the National Resource Center has highlighted the central importance of the first-year experience to higher education. As a result, many institutions around the world have come to recognize the value of focusing on first-year students and other students in transition and have begun to explore ways to better support their own first-years. The work of the NRC has emphasized not just the importance of initiatives directed toward first-year students but has also continued to highlight the relevance of research and evaluation about student transitions. Since the National Resource Center launched its first international meeting in 1986, several other meetings have emerged, demonstrating the relevance of this work in all higher education settings. In 1995, Queensland University of Technology hosted the first Pacific Rim Conference on the First Year in Higher Education, and the European First Year Experience Conference was launched in 2005. Most recently, the inaugural Southern African Conference on the First Year Experience in September 2008 met with great success. These meetings also highlight the growing number of initiatives being developed to support first-years and the increase in research on their particular experiences and needs.

This collection shows some of the exciting strategies that have been developed around the world and which have been subject to some **assessment** efforts. Each of the case study examples included are based on the core belief, aptly expressed by Gardner, Upcraft, and Barefoot (2005), that "first-year students can and will do better when placed in intentional intellectual and social campus environments that challenge and support their efforts to succeed" (p. 524).

The First-Year Experience as a Global Movement

Over the last 20 years, there have been a number of key research initiatives on the first-year experience. Early work in the USA by Upcraft, Gardner, and Associates (1989) has been particularly influential. Tinto's (1993) work on student retention, while focused on explaining student withdrawal, led to an influential conceptualization of first-year engagement. Dey and Astin (1989) also explored student retention and provided a way to understand student persistence through and beyond the first year by highlighting the role of individual student characteristics. Astin (1997) also emphasized the importance of understanding the role student retention plays in institutional decision making. Outside the USA, McInnis, James, and Hartley (2000) provided an exploration of first-year trends across Australia, and their work played a key part in an increasing focus on the first year in that country. Krause, Hartley, James, & McKinnis (2005) more recent work has provided an effective exploration of first-year experience in contemporary Australia by reviewing 10 years of national studies. In the UK, research by Yorke (1999) on student retention has been very significant in shaping thinking about first-years and other students in transition. He highlighted the complexity of withdrawal patterns among students and emphasized the role of institutions in understanding and responding to these departures. More recently in the UK, two major projects have been undertaken that focused on the first-year experience: (a) Harvey, Drew, and Smith (2006) provided a comprehensive literature review on the first-year experience and (b) Yorke and Longden (2007) completed a major research project that investigated first-year experiences across institutions in England and Wales.

In addition to these major projects, a range of smaller projects has also been undertaken. Harvey et al.'s (2006) literature review argues that much of this work has focused on individual institutions or on specific aspects of the first-year experience, specific student groups, or on particular initiatives. He suggests that we still need to research students' first-year experiences more systematically and more widely, particularly outside the USA. Nonetheless the research work that has been undertaken has identified a number of critical factors that need to be carefully considered by institutions and individuals involved in planning and supporting the first-year experience.

According to Tinto (1993), a fundamental concern for all higher education institutions is how to effectively integrate new students into their new learning environment. Tinto (1997; 2000) also suggested that making friends with other students also has a major impact on whether students stay and do well in their studies. He points out that we need to consider ways to change our institutions to better fit our students, rather than change the student to fit the institution. This argument has also been explored by Thomas and Cooper (2000). Using learning communities and initiatives to enhance interaction in the classroom have been identified as important ways to shift the focus of learning (e.g., Tinto, 1997; 2000). An important factor for many institutions is whether students are effectively prepared for higher education study. There is a growing concern in research and evaluation of institutional practice about the underprepared student (e.g., Astin, 1997; 2000; Du Pre, 2003). Both integrating the student and responding to their level of preparedness have led to a great deal of work in the UK, USA, Australia, and New Zealand exploring strategies to support student **induction** (see for example, Bourner & Barlow, 1991; Edward, 2003; Ward-Roof & Hatch, 2003).

Yet as an interest in the first-year experience has expanded around the globe, there have also been important adaptations to accommodate a range of different educational contexts. Over recent years, there has been a growing interest in the UK, Australia, and New Zealand in first-year students and strategies for supporting their learning and their engagement with university life. This has been set in the context of a different kind of higher education system than that in the USA, a primary difference being the normal length of study. While most students in the USA study for four years, in the UK and Australasia the norm is three years. This means that students in these latter countries are required to "hit the ground running." The concept of the first-year seminar, which works so well in the USA and in some other countries where four years is more typical, is not really compatible with the three-year model of study, which is heavily focused on the degree discipline from year one. This has led to a range of ideas and strategies designed to fit these limitations.

Another key difference that has shaped the global expansion of first-year initiatives is the level of participation. It is only in more recent years that the UK and Australasia have opened their doors to a wider range of learners. While the USA has had open enrollment institutions for a long time and, therefore, has had to consider the needs of diverse learners, it is only in the last 10 to15 years that this has been true for other major English-speaking nations. It is no coincidence that the increasing interest in first-year experience runs alongside this shift, as it did in the USA.

In other parts of the world, the first-year experience has been highlighted in different ways and at different times. Canada, Japan, South Africa, and many European countries (e.g., Belgium, Denmark, the Netherlands, Norway, the Republic of Ireland, Spain) have begun to explore strategies for engaging their first-years as their own demographics have changed, albeit for differing reasons. How students are funded, the impact of increases in the number of young people in a country, and government agendas for participation and for funding higher education are some of the factors that play a part in creating a climate where the interests of first-years are seen as important. The 2009 International Conference on The First-Year Experience included contributions from the Republic of Ireland, Spain, and Hong Kong, and previous conferences have had presentations from the Netherlands and the Caribbean. The European First Year Experience Conference has had contributions from Belgium, Denmark, the Netherlands, and Norway as well as the Republic of Ireland, and the 2009 Conference, held in Groningen in the Netherlands, had a particular focus on researching the first-year experience. The issues addressed at these international gatherings were varied: student support services collaborating with **academic staff**, pre-entry work to better prepare students for their studies, skills development for students in the first year, institutional first-year strategies, and first-year assessment. In recent years, these conferences have highlighted what we can know (and in some cases, need to learn) about our first-year students and what we might do to improve their experiences and promote their success.

Overview of the Monograph

The purpose of this monograph is to share good practice from around the world in enhancing the first-year experience and improving first-year student success. Because the higher education context determines the shape of first-year initiatives on campuses around the world, we open with an overview of higher education systems of the countries represented in the monograph. Here, we explore some of the differences and similarities between those contexts and note that it is not just policies and macro characteristics that explain the growing interest in first-year experience in various parts of the world. Rather, professors, tutors, researchers, and student support staff who work with first-year students continue to highlight their particular experiences and the real challenges they face in the transition into higher study. The overview is followed by 16 cases studies of initiatives designed to support the transition and success of first-year students. Each case includes a brief description of the institution and its students, an overview of the initiative, and a description of research-supported outcomes associated with the initiative. We conclude the volume with an essay identifying key points for consideration when designing first-year initiatives that arise from the case studies. To help readers navigate the unique terminology associated with these varying higher education contexts, we have also included a glossary of terms. Terms included in the glossary appear in bold the first time they are used in a chapter.

The examples of new and innovative work in this collection are drawn from 11 different countries and encompass a wide variety of institutional types and contexts. Some are research-intensive while others focus on teaching; some concentrate on traditional academic disciplines while the provision of others is strongly vocational. Both three-year and four-year institutions are represented, while one paper focuses on a two-year program. Some of the initiatives are institution-wide while others are discipline or department-specific. Some focus on curriculum change and development while others address broader issues of student support.

What they all have in common is a real concern for first-year students and a desire to see them succeed. All of the examples are strategies that we feel are transferable to other contexts and conditions. Each of them provides ideas for readers to consider in their own institutional contexts. All the initiatives have been evaluated, and the authors reflect on what they have learned, offering suggestions for future development and strategies for adapting the model to other contexts. The examples are an interesting mixture of approaches to making the transition into and through the first year a smoother one.

This collection is, in a sense, a snapshot. We have captured a moment in time, and included only a small sampling of the initiatives designed to support first-years. We know there is interesting work going on in countries not represented here – for example, in the Netherlands, in the Republic of Ireland, in the Unites Arab Emirates, in Norway, in Scotland (there will be some further mention of work going on in Scotland in the Overview of Countries), in Belgium, and in Jamaica. For some countries, we have only been able to include one example, and in each case we know there are other initiatives taking place in these countries. We trust that this other work will be shared and discussed at future conferences and in further publications. Meanwhile, we hope that this collection provides readers with an insight into some of the developing work going on across diverse contexts.

A brief description of the different strategies in the collection will demonstrate the range of practices and also be a helpful guide to reading the collection. O'Shea's Australian case study reports on transition to study workshops for new students, which are led by student mentors and provide new first-years with a short **orientation** program that focuses on empowering them and responding to their needs. The example from Canada, provided by Fisher-Stitt and Tam, is a peer-mentoring initiative in the Faculty of Fine Arts at York University. This initiative has received positive feedback from both mentors and those being mentored and has led to more confident first-years.

There are three examples from England, in the UK, which represent different approaches across different types of institutions. Teesside's case-study, provided by Nutt and Greer, reports on another institution-wide strategy, but here retention support officers in each **faculty** provide face-to-face support and guidance to new students, acting as a bridge to academic or pastoral help. The case study written by Ody and Carey from Manchester, a research-intensive institution, is an institution-wide approach focused on peer-assisted study (PASS). Here students help each other with their learning, not just with their integration into higher education. The third example is from Wolverhampton and highlights the value of new technological developments for supporting first-year students. Here, Purnell and Hughes explain their use of blogs to help new students engage with learning through writing.

Japan provides a case study in which Tanaka explores a peer community program at Kansai University, which is designed to help students develop their empathy and peer support skills. The program at Kansai has been developed to enhance students' communication skills and their ability to work with each other enabling them to integrate into the University, and both support and learn from each other.

The case study from Morocco provides an interesting example of implementing a first-year seminar, based on the University 101 course developed at the University of South Carolina in the USA. Ouakrime's initiative has impacted both student retention and the integration of first-year students into the institution.

There are two case studies from New Zealand. The first example from New Zealand is provided by Carson and Scarborough from Auckland University of Technology and focuses on providing proactive support for at-risk students through peer-support interventions. The second, from Clark at The University of Auckland, reports on the UniGuide program in which current students provide support and guidance to a group of new students for the first six weeks of their first semester. The group becomes a learning community so this initiative is somewhat different from an individual mentoring scheme.

In the one case study from Northern Ireland, Rushton and his co-authors describe a residential event used with environmental science students as part of their induction into university study. It highlights the importance of building relationships between students and between staff and students. While this example focuses on a particular discipline, the strategy is suitable for a variety of disciplinary contexts.

Rosário and his colleagues from Minho University in Portugal describe classroom activities designed to promote self-regulated learning. The activities focus on the discussion of six reflective letters written by a first-year student describing his experiences at the University. This comic account engages students and helps them explore their anxieties about studying in higher education and about the skills areas they need to develop.

The example from South Africa, provided by Botha and van Schalkwyk, describes the First Year Academy at Stellenbosch University, an institution-wide approach designed to foster student success. The Academy provides a range of strategies designed to underpin the first-year experience and was instrumental in ushering in a new attitude at Stellenbosch, making the first year an institutional priority.

Orvehed and Söderman, from Sweden, introduce us to the SciTech model at Uppsala University, which uses coaching to support new students and to encourage them to engage in the first year in both academic and personal terms.

Two case studies are included from the USA, from Portland State University and from Purdue University. Patton and Carpenter report on the Freshman Enquiry program (FRINQ) at Portland State. This is a three-term course, which encourages greater interaction between faculty and students and between students while supporting active learning. The example from Purdue University, provided by Koch and Drake, describes the work of the Student Access, Transition, and Success Programs department, which oversees the first-year experience across a very large and diverse institution. The department is the driver of a range of strategies supporting the enhancement of first-year experiences.

The final country represented in this collection is one of the smallest, Wales. Fitzgibbon and colleagues describe the Faculty Advice Shops at the University of Glamorgan, which provide drop-in guidance for students providing them with academic help and pastoral support. Each faculty has one and, in addition to providing support directly to students, these shops actively engage with the staff in the faculty to develop other initiatives that promote student retention.

We hope you find these case studies interesting and useful. They present a collection of good practice examples that we believe are transferable to other national and institutional contexts. Our aim is to share with you the work of colleagues around the world in the hope that it will inform and further enhance your own practice and, of course, benefit your own first-year students.

References

Astin, A. W. (1997). How "good" is your institution's retention rate? *Research in Higher Education, 38*(6), 647-658.

Astin, A. W. (2000). The civic challenge of educating the under prepared student. In T. Ehrlich, (Ed.), *Civic responsibility and higher education* (pp. 124-156). Westport, CT: Greenwood Press.

Bourner, T., & Barlow, J. (1991). *The student induction handbook.* London: Kogan Page.

Dey, E. L., & Astin, A. W. (1989). *Predicting college student retention: Normative data from the 1985 freshman class.* Los Angeles: Higher Education Research Institute, UCLA.

Du Pre, R. (2003, July). *Coping with changes in HE in South Africa*. Paper presented at FACE Annual Conference, Scotland. Retrieved November 15, 2007, from http://www.face.stir.ac.uk/documents/Paper101-RoyduPreR.pdf

Edward, N. S. (2003). First impressions last: An innovative approach to induction. *Active Learning in Higher Education, 4*(3), 226-242.

Gardner, J. N., Upcraft, M. L., & Barefoot, B. O. (2005). Conclusion. In M. L. Upcraft, J. N. Gardner, & B. O. Barefoot (Eds.), *Challenging and supporting the first-year student* (pp. 515-524). San Francisco: Jossey-Bass.

Harvey, L., Drew, S., & Smith, M. (2006). *The first-year experience: A review of literature for the higher education academy*. Retrieved January 10, 2007, from http://www.heacademy.ac.uk/4887.html

Krause, K. L., Hartley, R., James, R., & McInnis, C. (2005). *The first year experience in Australian universities: Findings from a decade of national studies*, Melbourne, Australia: Australian Government, Department of Education, Science, and Training.

McInnis, C., James, R., & Hartley, R. (2000). *Trends in the first year experience*. Canberra, Australia: DETYA Higher Education Division.

Thomas, L., & Cooper, M. (Eds.). (2000). *Changing the culture of campus: Towards an inclusive higher education*. Stoke on Trent: Staffordshire University Press.

Tinto, V. (1993). *Leaving college: Rethinking the causes of student attrition* (2nd ed.). Chicago: University of Chicago Press.

Tinto, V. (1997). Classrooms as communities: Exploring the educational character of student persistence. *Journal of Higher Education, 68*(6), 599-623.

Tinto, V. (2000). Learning better together: The impact of learning communities on student success in higher education. *Journal of Institutional Research, 9*(1), 48-53.

Upcraft, M. L., Gardner, J. N., & Associates. (1989). *The freshman year experience: Helping students survive and succeed in college*. San Francisco: Jossey-Bass.

Ward-Roof, J. A., & Hatch, C. (Eds.). (2003). *Designing successful transitions: A guide for orienting students to college* (Monograph No. 13, 2nd ed.). Columbia, SC: University of South Carolina, National Resource Center for The First-Year Experience and Students in Transition.

Yorke, M. (1999). *Leaving early: Undergraduate non-completion in higher education*. London: Falmer.

Yorke, M., & Longden, B. (2007). *The first-year experience of higher education: Final report*. York: Higher Education Academy.

Overview of Countries

Denis Calderon, Diane Nutt, Ludolph Botha, Wayne Clark, Kim Donovan, Norma Sue Fisher-Stitt, Rachel Frampton, Vicky Hill, Mary Stuart Hunter, Yuriko Kite, Kerri-Leigh Krause, Mohamed Ouakrime, Toshiya Tanaka, and Susan van Schalkwyk

We commissioned people from several of the countries in this collection to write an overview of their nation's first-year experience, and our own researchers investigated the key characteristics of the represented countries. Our interaction with the commissioned authors and the work of our researchers confirmed that direct international comparisons can be at best unhelpful and at worst very misleading. The definitions used for key first-year concerns and the measures of first-year performance differ considerably across contexts and are, therefore, not typically comparable. For example, some countries focus on retention and measure withdrawal rates, while others measure progression and completion and may not record withdrawal rates in any real way. The length of time a country uses to identify completion rates can also vary; one country might measure completion rates based on how many students complete in four years, another five years, and yet another seven. Other variations include institutional differences, course-specific differences, and varied social and financial factors. These differences in policy and practice mean that it is extremely difficult to compare patterns of student performance and concerns. Despite these limitations, we thought it useful to provide a context for reading the case studies and to provide some understanding of the wide variety of influences that shape the first-year experience in countries around the world.

The discussion begins with a consideration of the wider international context and is followed by an introduction to each of the countries represented in this collection. We look forward to more such developments in the future and seeing more countries taking a strategic approach to the first-year experience in their own contexts.

The Wider Context

In addition to research undertaken in individual countries, a useful source for beginning to understand the differences between countries in terms of their higher education systems in general is the Rand report on retention in higher education (van Stolk, Tiessen, Clift, & Levitt, 2007). According to van Stolk et al., countries often define the terms "retention," "attrition," and "completion" in different ways; and while most tend to focus attention on retention and completion rates, others concentrate on attrition. These rates also vary between countries due to differing institutional, course-specific, financial, and social factors.

The report suggests that there is some commonality of approach between countries, and many initiatives reflect the work of Tinto (1993) and others on academic and social integration. Increased attention is being paid in many countries to enhancing pre-entry information, peer mentoring, transition programs, skills training, professionalization of support staff and retention officers, and the creation of smaller learning communities. However, according to van Stolk et al. (2007), it is difficult to assess the effectiveness of these approaches as few evaluations have established their direct impact on student participation and retention, and the impact of individual initiatives can be difficult to identify when introduced in conjunction with other initiatives.

Further evidence from the Rand report on retention (van Stolk et al., 2007) suggests that many countries have policies aimed at disadvantaged groups although the specific nature of these groups differs between countries. A key example might relate to ethnicity where categorizing different ethnic groups and differentiating indigenous populations makes any real comparison extremely difficult (Thomas & Quinn, 2003).

Student age can also be a factor that differs between countries. For example, the majority of students entering higher education in Sweden are over 21, whereas in Japan and Portugal most new students are 18. Even where countries differentiate by age, some define mature entrants as being 21 and over, some 23 and over, and others 25 and over.

Where withdrawal (attrition) is measured and explored, there is a complex variety of factors that explain students' leaving higher education **courses** before completion including age at entry, wrong choice of course, transition difficulties, and financial burden. The factors involved in leaving are more alike across different countries than are the methods to measure student progress and success. However,

> non-completion of a degree does not mean that the skills and competencies acquired will be lost and are not valued by the labour market. This is particularly the case in Canada, where one year of study can provide students attractive opportunities for employment on the labour market. (OECD, 2009, p. 93)

This perhaps provides some explanation for "students' decisions to leave the education system before graduating" (p. 93). Similarly in Sweden, students can leave a tertiary program before completing it, join the labor market, and continue their studies in a work-based environment (OECD, 2009).

Some key differences to bear in mind when reading the following section, and the case studies in this collection, are:

- ◇ The entry requirements for participation in higher education, as this affects how prepared students are likely to be for higher education. Is the higher education system open-access, an elite or highly selective system, or is it somewhere in between?
- ◇ The length of full-time degree programs. Four-year programs allow students a more general introduction to higher education before beginning specialized study; three-year programs require students to "hit the ground running," making the experience for students and the challenges for **academic staff** somewhat different.
- ◇ The kinds of educational institutions available (e.g., universities, polytechnics, colleges) and the types of students served by those institutions
- ◇ Funding for higher education. Is there state funding for higher education, and under what circumstances is it available?
- ◇ The political agendas shaping higher education institutions and their policies

While it is important to be aware of these differences, it is also of value to highlight the commonalities between countries. An important characteristic of contemporary higher education in almost all the countries represented in this collection is the increasing role of women in universities. There is ongoing evidence that women are now outnumbering men in higher education and, according to some studies, out-performing them (e.g., HEPI, 2009; Högskoleverket, 2008; U.S. Department of Education, 2009). Only Japan has more men than women studying in the higher education system at the undergraduate level, and the OECD (2009) has noted that even there "The enrolment of women in bachelor and advanced degree study—while not yet at the level of men—has been increasing rapidly in recent years." It is perhaps worth noting though that despite this increase in women entering higher education, there remain some disciplines, for example science and engineering, and particularly in some countries, where men still outnumber women (ECU, 2008). It may be that the increase of women in higher education can partly be explained by the increasing number of nonscience subjects available to study. In the UK, for example, subjects allied to medicine (e.g., nursing, pharmacy) and education recruit far larger numbers of students into higher education institutions than in the past, and these subjects recruit women to a much greater degree than men (ECU). In Canada, the increase in women is seen as related to the increasing role of women in the labor market (AUCC, 2007). However, it is interesting to note that some countries are now concerned because fewer men are entering university and because their success rates are generally lower than those of female students, particularly at undergraduate level (Ferrier, Mortensen, & Sewell, 2009).

Most countries in this collection are also engaged with supporting the participation of underrepresented groups, and in particular those from local ethnic minorities and indigenous populations. There is also evidence that many countries in this collection are concerned with increasing the participation of young people whose parents did not attend higher education and who come from lower income groups, often defined as first-generation students. These factors impact the nature of the first-year cohort and what institutions do to engage students.

Regardless of whether countries are engaged in a widening participation agenda, student motivation remains a concern for the higher education sector. All of the countries represented in this collection are concerned about first-year students' preparation for university, the transition students are making into higher-level learning, and the accompanying lifestyle changes students experience (whether or not they are residential).

While they may use different language to explain or measure it, most of the countries in this study are concerned about student retention (or progression) and success. Japan is perhaps the only country with such a high completion rate that this is not the case. For a variety of reasons, countries are concerned when their retention or completion rates are low, or their attrition rates are high. First, where the state funds higher education to any degree the financial cost is an important issue, and this is highlighted in some countries by government targets, and in some cases specific funding, for retention and completion (as for example in Australia and the UK). Second, there is a social cost for the country as graduates and graduate employment play an important part in the status of a country. Third, there is a social, personal, and often financial cost to the individual student. A fourth cost, often overlooked in the literature and sector analysis, is the negative impact upon staff of student withdrawal or student lack of success. Many **lecturers** comment on how satisfying it is to see their students succeed and how sad and disappointing it is to see them leave early, or fail. Finally, research in a variety of countries (e.g., Australia, New Zealand, South Africa, USA, UK) has included large-scale surveys with first-year students asking them about their experiences and highlighting their concerns (e.g., American College Testing Program, 2009; Krause, Hartley, James, & McInnis, 2005; Yorke & Longden, 2008). All the countries included in this study are engaged with trying to address at least some of the issues raised by these surveys.

The National Context

In this section, we will consider the context in each of the different countries for which case studies are presented. Where possible, we will refer to the national data available, as it may provide some insight into the national higher education system, and discuss briefly key social or political features that shape the higher education context in that country. We will also provide a brief overview of the first-year experience in each country, highlighting key priorities, particular challenges, recent developments, and achievements. The country overviews vary in length partly depending on what data are available (e.g., Australia, the USA, and the UK have highly organized research efforts and, thus, larger data sets on which to draw) and on the length of time that the first-year experience, or student retention, has been a priority. Some of the countries represented in this collection are relatively new to this agenda and may not yet have a history of gathering relevant data.

Australia

As was suggested in the introductory essay, Australia has been a key player in researching the first-year experience and in developing strategies designed to support first-year students. Australia has 39 public higher education providers spread across its eight states and territories. These higher education institutions are funded by the federal government and typically offer a standard undergraduate degree of three to four years, depending on the program configuration. Postgraduate awards at masters and doctoral levels are also offered in each university. While there are many private providers of higher education, including two private universities, data in this profile pertain only to the public universities in Australia.

The most recent figures, representing 2007 student enrollments, show that there are 976,786 students in Australia's public universities. Of these, 230,218 (24% of the total) are commencing undergraduate students, an increase of 3% compared to the previous year, and 56% of incoming students are female. Almost three quarters (71%) of first-year students study full-time, with the vast majority (81%) studying in internal on-campus mode (i.e., attending classes on campus). Only 13% of commencing students are enrolled in external off-campus mode (i.e., as distance learners studying via computer or other technology). In a geographically large country like Australia, learning from a distance, primarily using e-learning with some paper-based materials, is growing in popularity, though this varies considerably by institution.

Just 1% of the commencing students in 2007 self-identified as being of Aboriginal or Torres Strait Islander heritage. Again, this figure varies by institution, but the numbers of students in this category remain extremely low. Students from low socioeconomic backgrounds, many of whom are first-generation students, represent a little more than 15% of the commencing student population in Australian public universities. Mature students (over 21 years of age) represent one third of the student population, while international students account for approximately 30%.

At the time of the 2006 census, 27% of 18-20 year olds in Australia were enrolled in a university program, while another 14% were enrolled in further or vocational education colleges or equivalent (Birrell, Healy, Edwards, & Dobson, 2008). The national progression rate for 2007 was 85% while the national attrition rate for undergraduate bachelor students who commenced in 2006 was 17%.

National policies encouraging mass higher education have had a significant impact on Australian universities, as has the widening participation agenda. These developments have implications for engaging and supporting first-year students, particularly those who are first in the family to attend university. Over the past decade, the strong Australian labor market has seen employment rates rise, with a concomitant relative decline in demand for university places from school-leavers. This trend is expected to reverse as the global financial crisis sets in. Mature age student numbers have also increased.

There are three current key priorities for the Australian higher education sector, particularly in relation to the first-year experience: (a) widening participation, (b) retention, and (c) quality.

Increasing the proportion of students from a range of equity groups is a priority for the federal government and for each university. Federal funding is allocated to encourage widening participation in each university, yet the proportion of students from low socioeconomic backgrounds entering universities over the last 15 years remains relatively static. Of particular concern is the unacceptably low participation rate of Indigenous students in Australian universities. Increasing the access and participation rates of these students in higher education is a national and institution-level priority.

A related priority is retaining students in higher education. This is particularly important for students at risk of failing. The federal government allocates performance-based funding to reward universities who demonstrate increases in student retention and progression through the undergraduate years. This is both an economic and a social priority for the nation.

The third priority is that of ensuring the quality of the first-year experience for all students. While it is important to widen participation and retain students in universities, it is equally important to ensure that the quality of their experience is optimal.

Each of the abovementioned priorities brings with it many challenges. First, the widening participation priority demands resources, along with innovative thinking and a willingness to push the boundaries in order to increase the access, participation, and success rates of those who are most disadvantaged. Challenges remain in terms of approaches to student recruitment, admissions policies, community and school engagement, and first-year curriculum design and **assessment**.

Retaining and engaging students is a shared challenge for university leaders, faculty, and support staff alike. The challenge grows as we welcome nontraditional students on our campuses, and as we strive to intellectually stimulate all our students, including those who are most able among the cohort. This challenge demands coordinated, university-wide approaches to all facets of the student learning experience.

Third, the challenge of enhancing and monitoring quality in the first year is one that underpins the success of all first-year initiatives. In Australia, increasing emphasis is being placed on evaluating the student experience through such mechanisms as the Australian Survey of Student Engagement. Robust evidence-based approaches to quality assurance and enhancement are key to addressing this challenge.

National interest in the first year was advanced by the federal government's decision to fund a series of five-yearly national first-year experience studies that began in 1994. The fourth of these studies will take place in 2009, providing 15-year trend data that will inform first-year policy and practice across the nation. This federal government support has played a key role in raising the profile of the first-year experience in Australia. Also influential has been the role of the federal government's policy on performance-based funding—through the Learning and Teaching Performance Fund—that rewards institutions on the basis of such indicators as good teaching and retaining students in the first year and beyond. Policies such as this have encouraged institutions to introduce a range of initiatives such as first-year transition programs and the like. The last decade has also seen a rise in the emphasis placed on scholarly approaches to analyzing and implementing first-year practices in Australian universities as the need for rigorous, research-informed policy and practice has increased. These developments ensure that, despite ongoing resourcing challenges, Australian universities continue to attach importance and value to the first year.

Canada

The Canadian higher education system is primarily publicly funded, and undergraduate full-time duration of study is usually four years. However, it is worth noting that presenting a national overview of Canadian universities and the first-year experience is difficult as education comes under the jurisdiction of 10 provinces and 3 territories, and each province takes a somewhat different approach to higher education. In 2006, there were 920,000 students studying in higher education institutions. According to 2007 data (AUCC, 2007), the participation rate in Canada is 24%. Of these, 76% were studying full-time. Mature-age students (defined as over 25) make up 15% of the full-time cohort, and 65% of those are studying part-time. More than half (57%) of students are female. A number of students complete only a year of study (CAUT, 2008), but according to OECD (2009), 70-75% of students complete their studies.

There is a growing awareness in Canada, shared by many other countries in this collection, that national and international employment changes are requiring a more educated workforce; therefore, increasing higher education participation plays an important role in national developments (Beach, Broadway, & McInnis, 2005).

Research by Finnie, Lascelles, and Sweetman (2005) suggests that "parental education plays an important role in determining who goes on to post-secondary education, and at what level, even after accounting for a wide range of other factors" (p. 16). Success also seems to be influenced by parental education, with those who are first-generation students doing less well in higher education (Finnie et al.). A variety of countries are working to increase participation by, and the success of, first-generation students, and clearly the first-year experience movement has a vital role to play in this regard.

According to Beach et al. (2005), the key issues concerning Canadian higher education are: "underfunding, student access, and faculty (staff) shortage." The funding issues, highlighted by Beach et al. suggest that students are faced with increasing tuition fees, and universities are required to make their money go further. This has important implications for first-year students. Beach et al. argue that it is likely to impact access and success as students choose not to take on debt and as families are expected to provide higher levels of support. Other countries are similarly affected by tuition costs and changing funding arrangements for universities (e.g., Australia, New Zealand, UK, and the USA), leading to concerns about students' taking on too much part-time work alongside study and greater pressures from both parents and students to make program choices career relevant.

In terms of student access, government commitment to increasing access has led to various approaches in terms of both research and strategic initiatives (e.g., Pelletier, 2008). Pre-entry work with students and with their schools and colleges is now an important part of the first-year initiatives in Canada.

Faculty shortage, according to Beach et al. (2005) is also a developing problem in Canada, with a high number of older staff approaching retirement age. The UK and Australia have also noted similar demographic concerns. A range of demographic issues plays a part in strategic approaches to supporting first-years. For example, in Japan, as we shall see, a declining population is influencing developments within higher education.

Japan

The higher education sector in Japan is a private/public mix, with 77% of institutions being private. This is a relatively new phenomenon with the increase in higher education institutions over recent years being primarily in the private sector (Oba, 2005). According to Arima (2003), the participation rate in Japan was at 40% in 2003, and other evidence suggests this rate is still increasing, with the most recent figures suggesting that it has reached 46%. Interestingly this is in the context of a decreasing number of young people due to demographic changes, which suggests that there is some element of widening participation taking place in Japan with approximately 20% of students being first-generation.

Japan has also experienced some consolidation in the higher education system in recent years. According to Clark (2005),

> In April 2003, a three-year plan of mergers began and at least 35 of Japan's 100 national universities have merged or are in the process of doing so. Between 2003 and 2004, the number of national universities dropped to 87 from 100. No merger plans have been announced by Japan's private universities, which are relatively autonomous of the ministry. The number of private universities continues to grow at a rate of approximately 16 a year.

This shift in patterns of national university enrollments tends to suggest that any increase in student numbers may be within the private sector.

The majority of students studying are entering higher education at the age of 18, and almost all are studying full-time (98%). While the number of female entrants to bachelor programs has increased significantly over the last 10 years, 60% of students are male (Newby, Weko, Breneman, Johanneson, & Maassen, 2009). Currently twice as many men go on to graduate school. Japan has a very low attrition rate (11%), and 80% of students complete their program within four years.

Entry into higher education in Japan is by examination (i.e., national exams or institution-specific admissions tests). The top universities tend to use the national exams as a filtering process, and only after potential students have passed these exams can they take the specific entry tests for that university. According to Clark (2005),

> Given the great lifelong advantage traditionally enjoyed by those who graduate from a top university [in Japan], the stakes and pressure associated with the admissions and examination process are very high. Many students who fail to gain admission to their preferred institution try again the following year and commonly devote themselves full time to the preparation process at private schools known as yobiku. Such students are commonly referred to as *ronin*, or masterless samurai. The ronin experience is so common in Japan that the Japanese education system is often said to have an extra year built into it.

As the case from Kansai University highlights, a key concern for the Japanese first-year experience is helping new students make the transition to higher education study, particularly in terms of academic and social literacy. Current social conditions in Japan, with small families and a decreasing number of young people, are putting pressure on recruitment. However, it is also producing young people who may not be very confident in large social groups and not fully prepared for the style of higher education teaching and learning.

Morocco

Morocco's higher education sector is made up of universities, schools of higher education, and technical colleges. Higher education is largely state funded. According to Touahri (2007), "The number of people enrolling in Morocco's institutions of higher learning is on the rise, benefitting from programmes to encourage students and to lessen their financial burden." As with most of the countries represented in this collection, the increase in participation rates makes a focus on the first-year experience particularly relevant.

The number of university students in Morocco is increasing by 8% annually, "with 289,000 students enrolled in higher education courses for the academic year 2007-2008 compared with 267,000 the previous year." (Touahri, 2007). However, according to Clark (2006), the demand for higher education places is leading institutions to increase entry requirements. So while postsecondary institutions are open to *baccalauréat* holders (i.e., persons who successfully completed relevant exams in various subjects at the end of secondary education),

> many subjects and institutions require that students also pass an entrance examination. Most institutions or faculties will also require that students have minimum grades in their proposed majors. Furthermore, some institutions will only accept students who have obtained their baccalauréat in the year of application for registration. These extra requirements have been introduced over the last 10 to 15 years as schools have become unable to meet the burgeoning demand created by the official Moroccan policy of open access for baccalauréat holders. (Clark, 2006)

Current data on students within the Moroccan education system is difficult to find; however, according to government statistics almost half of those who graduated in 2005-2006 were women (Ministry of Higher Education and Scientific Research, 2006).

According to Clark (2006), "The proportion of students required to repeat a year is high, especially in the first year of studies, and it is not uncommon for students to take more than six years to complete a four-year degree." Until relatively recently, higher education programs of study tended to be two years plus two years. The first two years leading to a *diplôme* or *certificat*, and the subsequent two leading to a *licence* or *maiîtrise* (Clark, 2006); therefore, a higher qualification equivalent to a bachelor's degree would normally take four years (if there were no repeat years). However, according to Clark (2006), since 2004 changes have been taking place in Morocco that involve shifting to a credit accumulation system with an expected three years for a bachelor's degree, with a further two years of study for a master's (resembling the model in many universities in the UK, Australia, New Zealand, and in some other European countries). However, not all higher education institutions in Morocco are currently using this new model.

Key concerns for the first-year experience in Morocco, then, are tensions around entry requirements, competition between institutions (Clark, 2006; Touahri, 2007), helping students adapt to a changing higher education system, and the consequences of higher education expansion (Touahri). As with many other countries in this study, there is also a concern about student preparedness for higher education (Ouakrime, 2003).

New Zealand

Despite its relatively small population and small number of higher education institutions, New Zealand has a strong commitment to supporting first-year students and a good reputation worldwide for effective first-year experience strategies. The higher education system is fairly similar to those in Australia and the UK; although, New Zealand uses the term "tertiary education" for postcompulsory education, which encompasses university and technical institute/polytechnic education, industry-based training, work-based training, and trade apprenticeships. Tertiary providers comprise 35 public institutions, including eight universities, 20 institutes of technology and polytechnics, and four colleges of education. Loader and Dalgety (2008) suggest that some of the diversity in tertiary study may benefit students who did less well in secondary education, as some of those with little or no qualifications from secondary school are doing low level certificates in tertiary, which may be "providing a way into education for students for whom school is not meeting their needs in some way" (p.4).

The majority of institutions in New Zealand are public and while students generally contribute 40% of the costs, 60% are publicly funded. The normal duration of bachelor degree study is three years although a variety of specialized bachelor's degrees require four years of study. Participation rate is fairly low (11%), with 54% of students being female and only two thirds (66%) of students studying full-time. More than half (57%) of students are over 25, with over 50% of these being part-time students. Only 61% of degree starters complete after eight years with first-year attrition at 33% (Smyth & Smart, 2008). Progression and completion are a national concern in New Zealand from both human capital development and financial investment perspectives and feature strongly in all tertiary education strategies.

Key challenges in New Zealand are perhaps primarily the high number of students (over 50%) over 24 who attend part-time, the high number of students (up to 55%) who are working more than 15 hours per week, and the increasing **Maori** and Pacific participation in a system where the highest rates of tertiary participation are by those who identify with the **Asian** ethnic group (33% of all students).

In a sense it could also be argued that contemporary New Zealand students are increasingly mobile and transient; spend little time on campus; use various and consistently changing technologies to communicate and gather information; are distracted by family, work, and lifestyle choices; and do not engage unless absolutely necessary. As a result they require a different campus environment than their predecessors. Yet, this description of New Zealand's contemporary students may sound familiar to educators in many Western countries.

Portugal

Higher education in Portugal and Spain is somewhat similar, and both are fairly typical of a traditional model of higher education replicated in various parts of Europe. The emphasis is on universities as research institutions that teach students who have relatively high-entry grades. There are some other institutions of higher learning that are more practically orientated, have less research activity, and more open access; however, according to Eurydice (2009), entry requirements are still relatively restricted (for a discussion about the binary nature of higher education in Portugal, see ENQA, 2006).

Universities and polytechnics can be public or private. While education in the private sector is increasing, the majority of students still study in a public institution (Strehl, Reisinger, & Kalatschan, 2007). The duration of Portuguese degree programs is a minimum of six semesters (three years), but programs normally last six to eight semesters (three to four years) depending on the field of study and institution (Eurydice, 2009).

There are slightly more women students than men (56% vs. 44%) according to Ivosevic (2007), but participation rates in Portugal are relatively low (about 9%) compared to other countries in this collection. Yet, these rates are comparable with several other European countries (e.g., Italy and Austria; OECD, 2007). According to the Portuguese Federal Ministry of Education and Research (2005), "Children from blue collar backgrounds are extremely underrepresented at institutions of higher education in Germany, Austria, France and Portugal (ratios between 0.4 and 0.5)" (p. 61). The majority of students in Portugal study full-time (81%) and is younger, with 82% being in the 18-24 age range (HIS, 2006).

A major concern for the first-year experience in higher education institutions in Portugal is the demographic change involving an aging population and a consequent reduction in the numbers of students entering university. This shift follows several years of expansion in the higher education sector and is exacerbated by concern about the success rates in upper secondary education (Ministry of Science Technology and Higher Education, 2006). There are also national concerns about the quality of higher education (ENQA, 2006) and about attainment rates (OECD, 2007). As in many other European countries, there is also a growing emphasis from the government on "broadening the qualification of the Portuguese population and its knowledge base in an international context" (Ministry of Science, Technology and Higher Education, p. 11).

South Africa

In post-apartheid South Africa, university learning has become available to a far wider range of students, with very diverse entry profiles. The majority of students are from White or Indian/Asian backgrounds, but a growing percentage are Black African or mixed race and are entering university with quite varied educational backgrounds.

Most of South Africa's institutions are publicly funded. Although there are a growing number of private institutions, these are generally not accredited to confer degrees unless in partnership with a public institution. Studying in South Africa is relatively expensive for students, although there is a National Student Funding Association, which is a government-sponsored funding scheme that supports students from disadvantaged backgrounds. There are 630,000 students studying in South Africa according to Scott, Yeld, and Hendry (2007). The participation rate is 16%, and 56% of students are female.

There appear to be little data on age at entry or on whether any students are studying part-time; however, a recent conference paper by Koetsier (2009) noted that a number of older (often over 30), female, first-generation students are choosing to study part-time and by distance learning, which is providing a particular challenge in terms of completion rates and first-year success. According to the Council for Higher Education (Scott et al., 2007), completion rates in general are low (about 44%), but there is a marked disparity between White and Black African students with Scott et al. suggesting a 30% difference in completion rates. There are a relatively high number of distance programs in South Africa (36% of registrations are for distance study), and these have a higher attrition rate than those based on campus (30% in the first year compared to 20%).

Key concerns in South Africa are shaped by changing political, social, and economic contexts. Engaging students from nontraditional backgrounds, particularly Black African students, and supporting students to succeed are major priorities. The issue of managing distance programs effectively is also a growing concern. In 2008, Stellenbosch University hosted the first Southern African First Year Experience Conference, which had a wide range of presentations and was very well attended, suggesting that the first-year experience is now a key concern in South African higher education.

Sweden

According to the Swedish National Agency for Higher Education, the participation rate in Sweden is very high and well above the OECD average (Högskoleverket, 2008). It is difficult to identify an exact number as the criteria used in Swedish data to describe participation is actually participation of those eligible, with The Swedish National Agency quoting 75%, while other data sources suggest participation rates overall are comparable with those in Australia. However, the level of participation probably indicates a very different approach than other European countries (e.g., Austria, France, Germany, Italy, Spain (OECD, 2007).

One of the reasons for high levels of participation in Sweden relates to funding. According to Forneng (n.d.), "Tertiary education in Sweden is almost 100 percent state funded. The institutions are paid per student at a rate that differs between subject categories. The students get financial support from the state and they have a right to special state guaranteed loans." Entry requirements may also be a factor. The main requirement for entry into higher education is successful completion of a nationally approved secondary education program. Alternatively, mature students are eligible if they are "25 years of age and have four years gainful employment" (Forneng). However, a number of courses require specific qualifications; for example, advanced courses in mathematics are required for programs in civil engineering (Forneng).

In Sweden, higher education is organized into short courses (usually of 5-20 weeks duration), and students accumulate credits from courses (at different levels) to achieve a degree. As a result, measuring retention and completion rates is difficult. About 70% of students are still registered after one year, although 10% of these are likely to have moved to a different institution. It has been suggested that a high number of mature students take only one or two courses. Full-time study is usually three years; however, professional programs often involve full-time study up to five years. A high number of students take a lot longer than this to complete their studies, using the credit accumulation system to build their degree program over longer time periods, which can include retaking some courses.

Women outnumber men in Swedish universities 61% to 39% according to Högskoleverket (2008), although participation rates vary across subjects. As Högskoleverket notes,

> In higher education, female and male students choose different programmes and specialisations. According to this source, during the last ten years women have dominated several study programmes. In seven out of ten broad subject areas, there are more female than male students who graduate and male students are only dominant in technical subjects. The graduation rate for women is higher in almost all the study programmes leading to vocational or professional qualifications. In recent years, women have also strengthened their position in the most prestigious study programmes.

There has also been an increase in the participation of under-represented groups in Sweden (Högskoleverket; Forneng, n.d.), and evidence suggests that those from lower socioeconomic groups are participating more fully in higher education.

Some of the key concerns impacting the first-year experience in Sweden are (a) the continuing increase of participation of under-represented groups, (b) the changing face of European higher education linked to the **Bologna Process** (where European institutions are looking toward a common credit accumulation model that will enable greater movement between countries in Europe and more comparable qualifications), (c) the increasing number of international students, (d) a lack of student preparedness for higher education, and (e) the need to help students cope with the complexity of higher education and complete their programs of study in a timely fashion (given their model of building credits). Examples of good practice in Sweden are often focused on these areas.

United Kingdom

The UK is made up of four countries: England, Wales, Northern Ireland, and Scotland. The four countries share many political and social processes, including the system by which students apply to enter university (UCAS, University and Colleges Admissions System) and, therefore, all institutions in all four countries are in competition with each other for students (and for staff). Thus, any good educational practice in one country is likely to have an impact beyond its borders. The first three countries are represented by cases in this volume. While the volume does not include a case from Scotland, a significant amount of work on the first year has taken place there in recent years, and it is worth mentioning some of this work, especially as it is likely to impact developments elsewhere in the UK. The Scottish quality approval system provides funding for investigating key aspects of higher education practice and the student experience. During the period 2005-2008, a particular focus of this investment was on the first-year experience, and the outcomes of this work will likely influence thinking and practice in the other countries in the UK and shape the future activities of the Quality Approval Agency (QAA) in England and Wales. For further information on the work in Scotland, readers should visit the QAA Scotland web site at http://www.enhancementthemes.ac.uk/themes/FirstYear/default.asp.

This work in Scotland has been possible because the Quality Approval Agency, which oversees all higher education programs on behalf of the government, works differently in Scotland than in other parts of the UK. However, despite not having this specific context to support the first-year experience nationally, the rest of the UK has been engaged with enhancing the first-year experience for some time in a variety of institutions. Perhaps this activity has been more localized because of necessity, but it still shows a groundswell of commitment to the first-year experience. Recent examples of a more cohesive approach can be seen in the work of the Higher Education Academy, which has funded both a major literature review (Harvey, Drew, & Smith, 2006) and a national survey of the first-year experience (Yorke & Longden, 2008). These projects both highlight examples of good practice in England, Wales, and Northern Ireland as well as further afield.

Statistics are usually measured either across the whole of the UK, or for England, Wales, and Northern Ireland together, with separate data produced for Scotland. Unless otherwise stated, all figures quoted here are for the whole of the UK. According to the Higher Education Statistics Agency (HESA, 2008), 39% of young people participate in higher education in the UK with 68% of all students studying full-time. A relatively high percentage of students are older, with 60% of students being over 21 on entry; however, most of these are studying part-time courses (95% of part-time students are over 21), only some of which will lead to a degree-level qualification. Because of this, most full-time undergraduate degree programs in universities have a relatively young cohort of students. More women than men are studying at undergraduate level in the UK (56% to 44%), but as noted in other countries, women and men also tend to be more heavily represented in different discipline areas. While women are in higher numbers in most areas, men are still in the majority in the sciences and engineering (ECU, 2008).

According to the National Audit Office (2007) report on retention in England, Wales, and Northern Ireland, 91% of first-year students continue into the second year, though not all within the same institution. Most degree programs in the UK are of three-year duration; although more recently, foundation degrees have been introduced in the UK, which take two years, and from which students can transfer to a bachelor's degree program if they desire. Foundation degrees resemble associate's degrees in the USA, although to receive funding from the government for foundation degrees, work-based learning must be a key requirement within the program. This highlights the emphasis in recent years in the UK on the role of higher education in education for, and within, employment.

Completion statistics are calculated based on completing bachelor's degree programs within four years. The overall completion rate is 79%; however, it is worth noting that retention and completion rates vary widely depending on institution, with elite, research-focused universities losing fewer than 10% of their students, while some colleges and modern universities, which tend to have far more open access, losing as many as 35%. The commitment of the national Higher Education Statistics Agency (HESA) to measuring retention in terms of the numbers and proportion of students completing the first year places considerable political and financial pressure on institutions.

Higher education in the UK is primarily state-funded. Most higher education institutions gain some funds from research and employment links, but this is a relatively small source of income for most institutions. A very small select group of research-intensive institutions gain the majority of their funds from other sources but still receive state funds for teaching students and for some research activities. State funding is primarily calculated around student numbers although a complex calculation takes place, where institutions can gain more funds for attracting and retaining nontraditional students. The UK has had a commitment to widening participation for some years, and consequently, according to OECD (2009) data, 45% of students are now first-generation. This is probably in part because universities can be both rewarded for opening access and retaining students and penalized for low recruitment of nontraditional students and/or high dropout rates. There is a tendency for institutions with more open access to have higher dropout rates, but this is not always the case.

Students in the UK apply for loans to support their studies, and these are paid back once students pass a particular earning threshold after graduation. Parents or family members often provide further financial support while those on low incomes can also receive some extra funding for their studies. Part of the cost paid by students goes directly to the university, and some institutions have allocated a percentage of these earnings into funded scholarships.

Key concerns impacting the first-year experience in the UK are widening participation, retention, student preparedness for higher education, and funding. In the UK funding arrangements for students have changed in the last few years, and it is perhaps too early to provide evidence for how this impacts the first-year experience, but it remains a key concern. One factor that plays a part in this is the role of part-time paid work in the life of students. There is growing evidence that many students, including those in their first year, are working relatively long hours in low-status paid work alongside full-time higher education study. Funding issues may also impact students' choices in relation to both institution selected and course studied. For example, more students appear to be applying to their local universities.

Many of the good practice strategies being developed in the UK are focused on helping underprepared and first-generation students, supporting retention, and motivating students who have multiple priorities.

United States of America

As we suggested in the introduction, the idea of the first-year experience as a key concern for higher education institutions began in the USA approximately 30 years ago (see for example Upcraft, Gardner, & Associates, 1989) and the national context does provide some useful insights into ongoing concerns for supporting and engaging first year students.

The United States of America's higher education system is large and diverse. According to the U.S. Department of Education (2009), 17,758,870 students were enrolled in more than 4,000 colleges and universities in fall 2006. Female students outnumbered males 57.3% to 42.7% (Chronicle of Higher Education, 2009). Most students attended full-time (61.7%) with the remaining 31.5% attending part-time (Chronicle of Higher Education). Data from a National Postsecondary Student Aid survey of 80,000 undergraduates enrolled at 1,400 institutions in 2003-2004 found more than one third of students (34.6%) were first-generation college students, meaning that one or both parents' highest level of education was high school or less (Chronicle of Higher Education).

Varied types of institutions exist to meet the diverse needs of today's students, including research-intensive universities, regional teaching-focused universities, liberal arts colleges, community and technical colleges, and proprietary schools. In 2005, the Carnegie Foundation reported that of the 4,391 institutions in the United States, 1,737 were public (state-supported) institutions; 1,746 were private, nonprofit institutions; and 908 were for-profit institutions (Chronicle of Higher Education, 2009).

Participation rates in the USA are high: 66% of high-school graduates enrolled in 2006, and 37.3% of 18-24 year olds in the United States were enrolled in college (Chronicle of Higher Education, 2009).

Most undergraduate degrees are designed to be completed in four years of full-time study, with some programs such as engineering and pharmacy requiring five years of study. However, many students work at least part-time to earn money to support their studies, and others leave college, work to earn money, and then return at a later time. Other students move from one college campus to another during their degree attainment process. For these and other reasons, many students take more than four years to complete their undergraduate degrees.

The American College Testing Program (2009) has tracked student attrition for many years. Their research indicates that retention rates vary by type of college. In 2008, 72.3% of first-year students returned for their second year at four-year colleges and universities, and 53.7% of first-year students re-enrolled for their second year at public two-year colleges. Degree attainment figures are lower, with 52.5% of students at four-year institutions earning a degree within five years of entry and 31.7% of students at two-year colleges earning an associate degree within three years of entry.

Funding for higher education in the USA is as diverse and complex as are the types of institutions. Many institutional budgets comprise funding from a variety of sources including tuition and fees paid by students; governmental appropriations; financial aid and scholarships provided for students by government agencies, institutions, and foundations; government and private foundation grants for research and scholarship; and contracts with business and industry to support various aspects of college operations. Additionally, many institutions have endowments that generate funds for additional operational support. It is perhaps worth noting that costs have been increasing fairly rapidly in recent years, which is key concern for the higher education community in the USA.

The National Center for Public Policy and Higher Education (2008) publishes an annual report entitled *Measuring Up: The National Report Card on Higher Education*, which provides some insight into the political and social factors influencing the higher education context in the USA. The report "provides the general public and policymakers with objective information they need to assess and improve postsecondary education" (p. 28). The performance categories outlined in this report reflect the major political and social factors influencing higher education from a national perspective. They include (a) student preparation for education and training beyond high school, (b) opportunities for students to enroll in education and training beyond high school, (c) affordability of higher education for students and their families, (d) completion rates measuring progress toward degrees in a timely manner, (e) the benefits that states receive from having a highly educated population, and (f) information about student learning as a result of higher education.

The first year of college is a critical year for students, and the transition from high school (or life before college for adult students) to the college environment is challenging. Many students find the changing expectations related to their responsibility, learning, and behavior difficult to manage. Faculty and staff at institutions realize that simple osmosis will not transform high school students to successful college students and, therefore, create programs to address transitional issues. Key priorities for students in the first college year are to successfully adjust to the demands of collegiate-level learning, to adjust to a new social environment, and to manage daily living skills as a more independent individual.

Over the past 25 years, higher education in the USA has devoted significant attention and resources to first-year transition issues at the institutional, state, and national levels. A variety of strategies have been introduced in higher education institutions in the light of this, which provide both curricular and extracurricular support for students. So, for example, programs for specific nontraditional students have been established. More collaboration between academic and student affairs/student services has evolved, and some institutions have begun to view the first college year comprehensively. Concurrent with this evolution, increased assessment efforts developed on individual campuses, and numerous national surveys have emerged that place special emphasis on entering students and their development over the first year. The resulting national data have helped individuals and institutions view the first year as a discrete unit of analysis. Attention to the first year by the regional accreditation associations has also elevated the importance of the first college year to institutional and governmental policy makers. Many initiatives developed on campuses and on a national level through the support of external funding agencies, including the federal government (e.g., National Science Foundation, the Fund for Improvement of Postsecondary Education) and private foundations (e.g., The Pew Charitable Trusts and Lumina Foundation for Education). Consequently, increased research and scholarship on the first year has proliferated and strengthened, and institutional efforts to assist students in the transition to higher education have multiplied.

Conclusion

This chapter has provided a brief introduction to the countries represented in this collection in order to highlight some of the common factors and distinctive characteristics of the first-year experiences in different countries but also to provide a context for the specific case studies that follow.

Despite the many differences between countries and institutions, there is considerable commonality of issues and concerns. These include major growth in student numbers, significant changes in the profiles and backgrounds of students entering higher education, questions about the preparedness of students, and funding issues. All of the cases were chosen because we believe that they demonstrate ways of addressing some of these challenges at institutional and program levels and, most importantly, are transferable to different contexts and conditions.

References

Arima, A. (2003, June). *The future of higher education in Japan*. The United Nations University Public Lecture, Third Annual Michio Nagai Memorial Lecture. Retrieved May 5, 2009, from http://www.unu.edu/hq/public-lectures/arima.pdf

American College Testing Program. (2009). *What works in student retention?* Retrieved February 13, 2009, from http://www.act.org/research/policymakers/reports/retain.html

Association of Universities and Colleges of Canada (AUCC). (2007). *Trends in higher education, Enrollment* (Vol 1). Ottawa, Canada: Author. Retrieved July 12, 2009, from http://www.aucc.ca/_pdf/english/publications/trends_2007_vol1_e.pdf

Beach, C. M., Broadway, W., & McInnis, M. (2005). Introduction. In C. M. Beach, W. Broadway, & M. McInnis (Eds.), *Higher education in Canada*. Montreal/Kingston: McGill-Queen's University Press. Retrieved March 11, 2009, from http://jdi.econ.queensu.ca/Publications/HigherEducation.html

Birrell, B., Healy, E., Edwards, D. & Dobson, I. (2008). *Higher education in Australia: Demand and supply issues – a report for the Review of Australian Higher Education*. Clayton: Centre for Population and Urban Research, Monash University.

Canadian Association of University Teachers (CAUT). (2008). *Almanac of post-secondary education in Canada 2008-2009*. Ottawa, Ontario: Author. Retrieved March 11, 2009, from http://www.caut.ca/uploads/2008_CAUT_Almanac.PDF

Chronicle of Higher Education. (2009). *The almanac issue, 2008-2009*. Retrieved February 10, 2009, from http://chronicle.texterity.com/chronicle/almanac200809/

Clark, N. (2005). Education in Japan, *World Education News & Reviews, 8*(3). Retrieved March 10, 2009, from http://www.wes.org/eWENR/05may/practical.htm

Clark, N. (2006). Education in Morocco. *World Education News Review, 19*(2). Retrieved May 7, 2009, from http://www.wes.org/ewenr/06apr/practical_morocco.htm#contents

Equality Challenge Unit (ECU). (2008). *Equality in higher education: Statistical report 2008*. London, UK: Author.

European Association for Quality Assurance in Higher Education (ENQA). (2006, November). *Quality assurance of higher education in Portugal: An assessment of the existing system and recommendations for a future system* (Occasional Papers, No. 10). Helsinki: Author. Retrieved March 12, 2009, from http://www.enqa.eu/files/EPHEreport.pdf

Eurydice (Executive Agency for Education Audiovisual and Culture). (2009, June). *Summary sheets on education systems in Europe: Portugal*. Retrieved July 27, 2009, from http://www.eurydice.org

Ferrier, F., Mortensen, T., & Sewell, T. (2009). *Boys and higher education: What is the problem?* Panel presentation at the 18th Annual European Access Network Conference, June 2009, York, England.

Finnie, R., Lascelles, E., & Sweetman, A. (2005). *Who goes? The direct and indirect effects of family background on access to postsecondary education*. (Analytical Studies – Research Paper Series). Retrieved March 17, 2009, from http://www.statcan.gc.ca/pub/11f0019m/11f0019m2005237-eng.pdf

Forneng, S. (n.d.) *International comparative research: Under-represented groups in tertiary education*. Stockholm, Sweden: National Agency for Higher Education.

Harvey, L., Drew, S., & Smith, M. (2006). *The first-year experience: A review of literature for the Higher Education Academy*. Retrieved January 10, 2007, from http://www.heacademy.ac.uk/4887.html

Higher Education Policy Unit (HEPI). (2009). *Male and female participation and progression in higher education* (HEPI Report Summary, No. 41), Oxford, UK: Author.

Higher Education Statistics Agency (HESA). (2008). *Performance indicators in higher education in the UK 2006/07*. Cheltenham: Author.

Hochschul-Information Systems (HIS). (2006). Data reporting module: EUROSTUDENT III (2005-2008). (Data Portal). Hanover, Germany: Author. Retrieved March 18, 2009, from http://iceland.his.de/eurostudent/report/choice.jsp

Högskoleverket (Swedish National Agency for Higher Education). (2008). *Swedish universities & university colleges short version of annual report, 2008*. Retrieved March 17, 2009, from http://www.hsv.se/download/18.6923699711a25cb275a80002979/0829R.pdf

Ivosevic, V. (2007). *HE through gender lenses in Europe*. Paper presented at ESU's 53rd Board Meeting, November 26, 2007, Vilnius, Lithuania. Retrieved March 18, 2009, from http://www.esib.org/index.php/Publications/conference-documents/45-board-meetings/316-esus-53rd-board-meeting

Koetsier, J. (2009, May). *The first year experience of part-time students in a South African university: Exploring student support links between first year orientation programmes and after hours support services*. Paper presented at the European First Year Experience Fourth Annual Conference, Groningen, Netherlands.

Krause, K. L., Hartley, R., James, R. & McInnis, C. (2005). *The first year experience in Australian universities: Findings from a decade of national studies*, Melbourne, Australia: Australian Government, Department of Education, Science, and Training.

Loader, M., & Dalgety, J. (2008). *Students' transitions between school and tertiary education* (2nd ed.). New Zealand: Ministry of Education. Available from http://www.educationcounts.govt.nz

Ministry of Higher Education and Scientific Research (DFC). (2006). *Formation des Cadres en chiffres – 2006*. [French & Arabic]. Retrieved July 12, 2009, from http://www.dfc.gov.ma/

Ministry of Science, Technology and Higher Education. (2006). *Tertiary education in Portugal: Background report*. Lisbon: Author. Retrieved March 19, 2009, from http://www.oecd.org/dataoecd/21/17/39710472.pdf

National Audit Office. (2007). *Staying the course: The retention of students in higher education*. London: The Stationary Office.

National Center for Public Policy and Higher Education. (2008). *Measuring up 2008: The national report card on higher education*, San Jose, California: Author.

Newby, H., Weko, T., Breneman, D., Johanneson, T., & Maassen, P. (2009). *Reviews of tertiary education: Japan*. Paris: OECD (Organization for Economic Cooperation and Development).

Oba, J. (2005, February). *Higher education in Japan: Incorporation of national universities and the development of private universities*. Paper prepared for Seminars on Higher Education, Istanbul and Ankara, Turkey. Retrieved March 11, 2009, from http://www.tr.emb-japan.go.jp/T_04/Education.pdf

Organisation for Economic Cooperation and Development (OECD). (2007) *Reviews of national policies for education: Tertiary education in Portugal*. Retrieved March 11, 2009, from http://www.oecd.org/document/14/0,3343,en_2649_39263238_39713934_1_1_1_1,00.html

Organisation for Economic Cooperation and Development (OECD). (2009). *Highlights from education at a glance, 2008*. Retrieved March 10, 2009, from http://browse.oecdbookshop.org/oecd/pdfs/browseit/9609011E.PDF

Ouakrime, M. (2003). Higher education in Morocco. In D. Teferra & P. G. Altbach (Eds.), *African higher education: An international reference handbook* (pp. 449-461). Bloomington, IN: Indiana University Press.

Pelletier, Y. Y. (2008). Testing ways to increase access to tertiary education: Canada's Future to Discover pilot project. In F. Ferrier & M. Heagney (Eds.), *Higher education in diverse communities: Global perspectives local initiatives* (pp. 51-59). London, UK: European Access Network.

Portuguese Federal Ministry of Education and Research. (2005). *Eurostudent report 2005: Social and economic conditions of student life in Europe*. Hanover, Germany: Hochschul-Information Systems. Retrieved March 17, 2009, from http://www.bmbf.de/pub/eurostudent_report_2005.pdf

Scott, I., Yeld, N., & Hendry, J. (2007). *Higher education monitor: A case for improving teaching and learning in higher education*. Pretoria: Council on Higher Education.

Smyth, R., & Smart, W. (2008) *Measuring up: How does the New Zealand tertiary education system compare?* New Zealand: Ministry of Education. Retrieved February 12, 2009, from http://www.educationcounts.govt.nz

Strehl, F., Reisinger, S., & Kalatschan, M. (2007). Country study: Portugal. *In Funding systems and their effects on higher education systems* (OECD Education Working Papers, No. 6). Paris: Organisation for Economic Cooperation and Development.

Thomas, L., & Quinn, J. (2003). *International insights into widening participation: Supporting the access of under-represented groups in tertiary education* (Final Report). Stoke on Trent: Institute for Access Studies.

Tinto, V. (1993). *Leaving college: Rethinking the causes of student attrition* (2nd ed.). Chicago: University of Chicago Press.

Touahri, S. (2007). *New initiatives boost higher education in Morocco*. Retrieved May 7, 2009, from http://www.magharebia.com/cocoon/awi/xhtml1/en_GB/features/awi/features/2007/09/30/feature-01

Upcraft, M. L., Gardner, J. N., & Associates. (1989). *The freshman year experience: Helping students survive and succeed in college*. San Francisco: Jossey-Bass.

U.S. Department of Education. (2009). *Table 191.* Washington, DC: National Center for Education Statistics. Retrieved February 13, 2009, from http://nces.ed.gov/programs/digest/d07/tables/dt07_191.asp

van Stolk, C., Tiessen, J., Clift, J., Levitt, R. (2007). *Student retention in higher education courses: International comparison.* Santa Monica, CA: Rand Corporation.

Yorke, M., & Longden, B. (2008). *The first-year experience of higher education in the UK: Final report.* York, UK: Higher Education Academy.

AUSTRALIA

Uni-Start: Student-Led "Transition to Study" Workshops

The University of Newcastle

The Institution and Its Students

The Ourimbah Campus is a joint venture between The University of Newcastle and the Hunter Institute of Technical and Further Education (TAFE) and offers programs that range from certificate level to doctorate. In 2008, there were 3,000 University and 3,500 TAFE students enrolled, and each year approximately 1,000 students commence university studies. In 2007, 60% of the University's entrants were termed mature-age (i.e., over 21 years of age), and more than 50% of all students were female. At the Ourimbah Campus, only a small percentage of students live on campus (in a 25-room hall of residence); the rest commute from the surrounding suburbs or the two closest metropolitan areas (i.e., Sydney and Newcastle).

The campus is located on the Central Coast region, which is recognized as both economically and socially disadvantaged. According to the most recent Australian Bureau of Statistics data (2001-2003), the area also has much lower university attendance rates than state or national figures (2% compared to 4% for state and national) as well as a much lower proportion of residents who have completed a university degree (6% compared with 11% for the state and 10% for the country) or completed the final year of high school (27% compared to 38% for the state). This demographic profile is reflected in the student population of The University of Newcastle where 27.9% of students are in the lowest socioeconomic band; this is the highest rate of SES disadvantage of any higher education institution nationally. The University also has higher access and participation rates for indigenous students compared to both state and national figures. However, the larger student population is not very ethnically diverse, which reflects the monocultural nature of the primary catchment areas. In 2007, fewer than 1% of students had a first language other than English, and 10.5% of all students were classed as international on-shore students (i.e., those students studying at a domestic campus of the University but under the auspices of an international student visa).

The Initiative

The low participation and success of certain equity groups within the Australian tertiary landscape has been recognized, with figures indicating that the percentage of students from a low socioeconomic status accessing university remained largely unchanged from 1993 to 2003 (James, 2004). The aim of the Uni-Start – Transition to Study Workshops was to ease the transition process for commencing University students at the Ourimbah Campus by providing two days of **orientation** activities designed to assist them in their transition to higher education study. While the program was open to all commencing University students, data have been collected on those deemed as being low SES. In both 2007 and 2008, more than 60% of participants identified as being in receipt of pensions or social security support (i.e., government assistance). The program is advertised in the Orientation Week schedule of events as optional; however, in both 2007 and 2008, it attracted between 10% - 15% of the commencing student population at this campus.

The difference between Uni-Start and other orientation programs is that the sessions are designed, developed, and facilitated by student mentors, who worked collaboratively with staff in the Learning Development Service. This program grew out of the recognition that students encounter difficulties and obstacles before formal commencement (i.e., matriculation), which then result in some degree of disenchantment and disappointment. For example, interviews conducted with first-in-the-family students indicated how initial expectations did not reflect reality (O'Shea, 2007). The Uni-Start program sought to dispel such misconceptions by presenting the university culture and environment from a student perspective as student mentors drove the content of the sessions. By offering the sessions during Orientation Week, the objective was to assist students in a timely fashion, providing not only academic skills orientation but also the opportunity for social interaction.

Some of the sessions were designed specifically to orient the students to the campus both geographically (e.g., scavenger hunt/Trivial Pursuit) and culturally (e.g., academic panel/guest speakers). In terms of academic skills, participants were given the opportunity to prepare an oral presentation and were provided with tips on time management, study skills, and essay writing. However, the student facilitators also included information on areas where they themselves had struggled. For example, assignment cover sheets were deciphered, and a definition activity was designed to explain university terminology. One of the additional strengths of the program was that all the sessions used authentic materials as student facilitators provided examples of personal study planners, essay plans, and notes. Indeed, it is this authentic aspect of the program that is one of its strengths, lending further immediacy and credibility to content.

The benefits of peer involvement in the transition of students have been well-documented in current literature on student learning and engagement. Research conducted by Yorke and Thomas (2003) indicates that information about university and academic skills are better received from student tutors, due to their age and stage of study. Equally, McInnis, James, and Hartley (2000) highlight how interactions with peers can facilitate the creation of successful student communities, while Kantanis (2000) suggests that peer interaction and networks can aid the transition and retention of first-year students. As Kantanis argues "...social transition underpins a successful academic transition to university." Kantanis' research indicated that the creation of peer friendships significantly impacts persistence; thus, the Uni-Start program also offered the space and opportunity to develop such relationships.

Research Design

In 2007 and 2008, the Uni-Start program was assessed through student evaluation forms containing a number of open-ended questions related to the quality of sessions and how information matched prior expectations. Each of the forms contained an invitation to be contacted for a further evaluation five weeks after commencement in order to gauge the impact of the program on student experience. Each of the student facilitators also wrote a reflective review, highlighting the personal and public impacts derived from creating and facilitating this session. Hence, the research has a dual objective both highlighting the initial effects of these sessions on first-year students and also outlining the outcomes for those students involved in actually delivering the program. Evaluation forms and reflections were analyzed thematically, the responses generating rich descriptive data.

Findings

In 2007, a total of 120 commencing students participated in the sessions. The evaluation was completed by 77 students, and more than 95% of them were either satisfied or very satisfied with the structure and presentation of the sessions, while 78% "strongly agreed" that the workshop had a clear relevance to their first-year studies. In 2008, the numbers of students participating in the Uni-Start program increased to 176. The evaluations were completed by 104 students, and again, students were satisfied with the course: 91% of respondents perceived attendance as "very beneficial" to their first-year experience. When the open-ended questions were analyzed, it became clear that students appreciated the blend of academic skills and social interaction. In highlighting, "the most useful aspects of the course," students noted the following:

> "….study skills and just the course itself allowed me to get to know new people and **lecturers**" (2007)

> "Being able to ask questions, meeting other students, and comparing how we felt about starting Uni" (2007)

> "Thank you for giving first-time students the opportunity to orientate, associate with other first timers, meet concerns and needs, a small taste of what's to come…" (2008)

Many of the comments made reference to increased levels of confidence and the fact that sessions enabled students to ask questions. In 2007, more than 20% of the responses specifically mentioned the question and answer (Q&A) session with lecturers as being beneficial, so this session was expanded in the following year to include more **academic staff** and an opportunity to socialize with panelists after the session. Thomas (2002) argues that in order to promote inclusivity within the university environment, academics should consider extending the limits of professional identity beyond the lecture hall and communicate with students in order to encourage positive self-esteem and personal growth. The need for such support has been borne out by the extensive literature and research that emphasizes the importance of the connection between student and lecturer, particularly in relation to academic persistence and retention (Elliott, 2002-2003; Perry & Allard, 2003; Scanlon, Rowling, & Weber, 2007; Shelton, 2003; Tinto, 1998). While the concept sounds easy, such connections are often not facilitated or supported within existing institutional frameworks. However, the informal Q&A sessions in the Uni-Start program offer such an environment, and this process is enhanced by scheduling the session on the second day when students feel more comfortable with each other and the location.

In addition, a number of students mentioned how helpful it was to recognize that "...everyone is in the same boat of uncertainty, discovering that everyone has the same fears..." At the same time, references to university being less daunting were also prevalent. Howells (2003) argues that one of the most "disorientating" experiences for first-year students, particularly those who are older or culturally diverse, is the lack of voice or recognition given to existing knowledge or sense of self. Moreover, Howells suggests that "if our assessment of the value of orientation programs is dominated by students' performance on future tasks we may miss the very questions and answers that are needed to assist students to get off to a good start" (p. 12).

The Uni-Start program sought to position beginning students as knowledgeable and, thus, empowered to recognize the skills and knowledge they bring to the learning experience. Instead of focusing on the acquisition of atomized skills, the activities highlighted the connection between university skills and life skills as well as imparting information at a grass-roots level.

Undoubtedly, this process was assisted by the key role played by the student facilitators who designed and wrote the content of sessions. The reflections written by the facilitators revealed how their involvement had enhanced their engagement with the University and how their confidence had improved. One of the facilitators explained how participating had "been a wonderful journey" and "enabled me to see just how capable I really am... [providing]... me with the opportunity to acquire professional skills valued by the University, the community, and employers." Another mentioned how she had encountered a student a few weeks later who explained how the program had assisted her in writing the first assignment, highlighting how "without it she may have found it all too daunting and left." The facilitator then concludes: "This to me is validation of the success and ongoing need of the program, for if this is indicative of one student's struggle, how many more have been assisted to stay?"

The second set of questionnaires sent out in 2007 yielded little further insight. While 40% were returned, this represented only 20 questionnaires. All mentioned that the program was beneficial in those initial weeks of study providing a greater understanding of academic expectations, locations of services, and "where to get help!" In 2008, the initial evaluation also contained an invitation to be contacted further to participate in small student focus groups planned for the end of the first semester. We anticipate that the focus groups will provide more in depth information.

Implications and Future Directions

Open-ended questions on both the 2007 and 2008 evaluations revealed a need for more discipline-specific information. Overall, 16% of the respondents mentioned this need:

"I would have appreciated a lecturer being here from each degree." (2007)

"It would be better if we were put in our degree [groups], e.g. all Early Childhood students together – meet the people in your course." (2007)

This then is the challenge for the Uni-Start – Transition to University program for the future: to embed this program within academic faculties. Indeed, this reflects a current theme in literature on student transition, the latest report on the Australian First Year Experience project indicates that orientation programs with an affiliation with faculty or academic department are more successful than those applied on a generic basis (Krause, Hartley, James, & McInnis, 2005). In 2008, the Uni-Start program was adopted by the Faculty of Business and Law and attracted more than 300 commencing students. Embedding the program at this **faculty** level is assisted by the presence of a strong mentor program (Stone, 2000) and by the fact that each Uni-Start initiative is tailored by student facilitators to meet the needs of the students within the targeted faculty. This process retains the relevance and currency of these activities.

There are always challenges in developing campus-wide first-year transition programs, particularly when the support and retention of students is traditionally regarded as being the responsibility of student support services. Mandel and Evans (2003) refer to the difficulty in instigating programs that do not seem to have academic support or rigor; if programs are not perceived to be integrated into faculty, then students may regard them as peripheral rather than central to their studies. However, commencing students need to be more effectively oriented to the realities of the university environment and who better to do that than their university peers. Overall, the ownership of this program lies with the students themselves and this, to me, is the major strength of this approach. The student voice is powerful in its immediacy and veracity; hence, as university educators, we should endeavor to not only listen but also provide spaces for students to be heard.

References

Elliott, K. (2002-2003). Key determinants of student satisfaction. *Journal of College Student Retention, 4*(3), 271-279.

Howells, K. (2003, July). *The first year experience: Starting with the student.* Paper presented at the 7th Pacific Rim, First Year in Higher Education Conference, Queensland University of Technology, Brisbane.

James, R. (2004). *Socio-economic background and higher education participation: An analysis of school students' aspirations and expectations.* Canberra: AGPS.

Kantanis, T. (2000). *The role of social transition in student's adjustment to the first year of university.* Retrieved September 4, 2003, from http://www.adm.monash.edu.au/transition/research/kantansis3.html

Krause, K.L., Hartley, R., James, R., & McInnis, C. (2005). *The first year experience in Australian universities: Findings from a decade of national studies* (Government Report). Melbourne: Centre for the Study of Higher Education.

Mandel, R. G., & Evans, K. (2003, March/April). Firstchoice: Creating innovative academic options for first-year students. *About Campus, 8*(1), 23-26.

McInnis, C., James, R., & Hartley, R. (2000). *Trends in the first year experience in Australian universities.* Canberra: Department of Education, Training and Youth Affairs.

O'Shea, S. E. (2007). Well I got here…but what happens next? Exploring the early narratives of first year female students who are the first in the family to attend university. *Journal of Australian and New Zealand Student Services Association, 29,* 36-51.

Perry, C., & Allard, A. (2003). Making the connections: Transition experiences for first-year education students. *Journal of Educational Policy, 4*(2), 74-89.

Scanlon, L., Rowling, L., & Weber, Z. (2007). "You don't have like an identity…you are just lost in the crowd": Forming a student identity in the first-year transition to university. *Journal of Youth Studies, 10*(2), 223-241.

Shelton, E. (2003). Faculty support and student retention. *Journal of Nursing Education, 42*(2), 68-76.

Stone, C. (2000). The SOS program (Students for Other Students): A student mentor program. *Journal of Australian and New Zealand Student Services Association, 16,* 55-74.

Thomas, L. (2002). Student retention in higher education: The role of institutional habitus. *Journal of Education Policy, 17*(8), 423-442.

Tinto, V. (1998). Colleges as communities: Taking research on student persistence seriously. *The Review of Higher Education, 21*(2), 167-177.

Yorke, M., & Thomas, L. (2003). Improving the retention of students from lower socio-economic groups. *Journal of Higher Education, Policy and Management, 25*(1), 63-74.

Contributor

Sarah O' Shea
Manager, Transition and Retention Unit
The University of Newcastle
NSW
Australia
Phone: (02) 4348-4395
Fax: (02) 4348-4065
E-mail: sarah.oshea@newcastle.edu.au

CANADA

Enhancing Performance: The Effectiveness of a Faculty of Fine Arts Peer Mentoring Program

York University, Toronto

The Institution and Its Students

York University is a publicly funded university situated in Toronto, Canada. The third largest university in Canada, York has a population of approximately 46,000 undergraduate students and 5,000 graduate students across 11 faculties. Females comprise 62% of the undergraduate population, and 84% of the students are pursuing their studies full-time, defined as taking a **60% course load**. Toronto is acknowledged as one of the world's most multicultural cities, and the York student population reflects the city's diversity: 82% of undergraduate students are Canadian citizens with the remaining 18% coming from 174 other countries; 41% of first-year students are first-generation (i.e., neither parent attended university); and 64% of first-year students live at home with a daily commute to school of 40 or more minutes each way. The majority of students are under age 25 (80%), but 17% of the student body falls in the age range of 25 to 50 years.

The Initiative

The Faculty of Fine Arts at York University houses 2,756 full-time undergraduate and 217 part-time undergraduate students across six units (design, dance, film, music, theatre, and visual arts). The Fine Arts Peer Mentoring Program, launched in 2006, was created to support first-year students in maximizing their academic and social experience. All first-year students face challenges for many reasons, both academic and personal, but students in the fine arts experience unique stressors, including performance and competition anxiety as well as significant time management issues. Matching first-year students (mentees) with successful upper-year students (mentors) in their own artistic disciplines enables mentees to receive peer guidance from someone who has successfully managed the transition into university.

At the end of each academic year, students with a minimum B average entering year 3 or 4 are invited to participate in the program as mentors. In their letter of invitation from the dean, they are told about the program and the commitment required of a mentor. Mentors participate in a structured training program delivered by the Faculty of Fine Arts Student and Academic Services staff as well as by experts from various University service areas such as the Counselling and Development Centre. The training program focuses on communication skills, knowledge of campus resources and support services, stress management, time management, motivation, and life skills. During the academic year, mentors are expected to meet one-on-one with their mentee(s) for at least one hour per week, to attend mentor/mentee forums and "coffee house" sessions, and to volunteer two hours per week in the Peer Advising Centre. Here, they work with other mentors advising fine arts students on a drop-in basis, answer the help line, respond to e-mail inquiries, and contribute to the mentor/mentee blog. At the end of the academic year, the mentors attend a special reception where they receive completion certificates from the dean and hear from selected Faculty of Fine Arts alumni on "Mentoring for Life."

Research Design

In 2007-2008, the Fine Arts Peer Mentoring Program was evaluated qualitatively through the administration of surveys and quantitatively through analysis of institution-level student data and National Survey of Student Engagement (NSSE) data. There were 822 students in the 2007 fine arts entering class, of whom 188 (23%) elected to participate in the peer mentoring program, 675 met the criterion of less than 30 credits completed for assessing GPA[1], and 172 completed NSSE surveys. The two principal questions driving the research were

1. Does participation in the peer mentoring program have an impact on the academic performance of first-year fine arts students?
2. Are there nonacademic benefits for first-year fine arts students who participate in the peer mentoring program?

Findings

In 2007-2008, we did an analysis comparing the mean grade point average of first-year students who had a mentor with the mean grade point average of first-year students who did not have a mentor. Students who had a mentor performed better academically than students who were not in the mentoring program, earning GPAs approximately one grade point higher (Table 1). Additionally, first-year fine arts students with mentors completed more courses (27.74 credits vs. 25.60 credits for students without mentors). Many students at York carry less than the 30-credit full course load because of their commuting times and the pressure to work. The high average of courses completed by those with mentors bodes well, indicating that the majority should graduate at the end of four years.

A review of the academic decisions for all first-year fine arts students at the end of the 2007-2008 academic year ($N = 822$) indicated that 3.6% ($n = 30$) of students in the first-year class were placed on academic probation (defined as those achieving a GPA under honors standing of 5.0 or C+). No first-year fine arts student with a mentor (23%, $n = 188$) was placed on academic probation.

Table 1

Impact of Mentoring on GPA

	FFA students < 30 credits completed	
	Mentor (*n* = 143)	No mentor (*n* = 532)
Major GPA	6.48	5.67
Overall GPA	6.19	5.32

Note. In the York scale, 5 is equivalent to a C+, 6 is equivalent to a B, 7 is equivalent to a B+.
p < 0.0001

Finally, the first-year fine arts students who participated in the peer mentoring program responded more positively than their colleagues without mentors and other first-year York University students on a number of NSSE questions (Table 2). The NSSE responses from first-year fine arts students with mentors indicate that the benefits of access to a mentor appear to extend beyond improved academic performance to include being more comfortable interacting with others and being more adventurous than their first-year peers.

Table 2

Responses to Selected NSSE Questions

NSSE question	First-year fine arts students		All first-year students (*N* = 1,742)
	Mentor (*n* = 46)	No mentor (*n* = 126)	
Often asked questions in class	32.7%	25.6%	23.7%
Very often worked with classmates outside class	30.0%	27.6%	11.5%
Often discussed ideas from class with others outside class	50.0%	33.3%	31.9%
Very often had conversations with students very different from themselves	35.6%	31.5%	26.4%
Had done community service or volunteer work	35.6%	24.8%	28.2%
Planned to study abroad	60.0%	45.8%	41.3%
York very much helped them to think critically and analytically.	48.9%	45.2%	39.0%
York very much helped them to develop personal values and ethics.	31.0%	25.9%	20.7%

Qualitative data have been collected in both years of the program (2006-2007 and 2007-2008) to assess other aspects of the student experience. Surveys with open-ended questions were distributed twice during the year, at the mid-point and at the end, to both mentors and first-year students. In their survey responses ($n = 30$), mentors highlight the benefits of the program for themselves. For example, 94% of the mentors stated that they not only learned new mentoring strategies but also that that what they had learned in the training sessions had helped them in their mentoring role. They indicated that the most useful training was in the area of stress and time management. Other comments included: "I learned that mentoring a fellow student helped me to grow as a person and an artist as I learned valuable communication skills that I can continually build on," and "One of the best programs I've had the privilege to participate in throughout my four years at York."

In their survey responses, first-year students acknowledged that having a mentor was beneficial in many ways, including: "I loved having a mentor as I felt more confident and learned more than just from my courses." The increased confidence expressed by this student was reflected in the NSSE responses by students with mentors.

Implications and Future Directions

Our goal for the mentoring program is to support first-year Faculty of Fine Arts students in their transition to university and to the academic and social experiences unique to postsecondary students with majors in the fine arts. The analysis of grade point averages after the first year indicates that students with mentors performed better than those without mentors. It is important to note that the entering grade 12 final averages for those students who elected to have mentors was only slightly higher (84.8%, $n = 156$) than the entering grade 12 average for those who did not opt to have a mentor (83.3%, $n = 684$). Given the positive results apparently associated with having a peer mentor, we are now more proactive in encouraging entering students to sign up for the program. For 2008-2009, we had a significant increase in the number of students applying for mentors (37% compared with 23% of the 2007 first-year class). Interestingly, upper-year students are also becoming increasingly aware of the benefits of involvement in the program, with the result that we had 125 mentors in 2008 compared with 65 in 2007.

The anecdotal feedback from the mentee and mentor groups indicates that involvement in the Peer Mentoring program has a positive impact on their overall experience as a student in the **faculty**. Mentors indicated that volunteering in the Peer Advising Centre provided them the opportunity to interact with students from other fine arts disciplines for the first time. This interdisciplinary interaction has resulted in artistic and academic collaborations.

We have retained the basic training structure of the program for 2008-2009 but have added more discussion groups with guest speakers, providing increased opportunities for meetings between mentors and mentees. This year, we also are introducing a Senior Mentor training program, which offers in-depth leadership and communications training to a group of 12 senior students who have already completed the existing mentor training. They will be mentoring a group of 20 second- and third-year students who are experiencing serious academic difficulty. In addition, the senior mentors will be matched with successful Faculty of Fine Arts alumni to enhance their own experience of being mentored as they prepare to embark on their lives and careers beyond university. In 2008-2009, alumni involvement extended beyond the Senior Mentoring program to include several key events such as a speed-mentoring evening, a discussion forum on "Mentoring for Life," and an end-of-year celebration that focused on mentoring and career planning.

The Faculty of Fine Arts Peer Mentoring program has been an enriching experience for all participants, including staff and faculty members. Through the forum of the York University

Retention Council, we have shared the details of our mentoring program with other faculties across the university, and we plan to collaborate so that first-year students in all faculties will have access to mentoring opportunities.

Notes

[1] At York University, the usual maximum full-time course load is 30 credits over the fall and winter terms.

Contributors

Norma Sue Fisher-Stitt
AVP Academic Learning Initiatives
York University
4700 Keele Street
Toronto, ON Canada
M3J 1P3
Phone: 416-736-5770
Fax: 416-736-5787
E-mail: normasue@yorku.ca

Lynda Tam
Director Academic Affairs, Faculty of Fine Arts
York University
4700 Keele Street
Toronto, ON Canada
M3J 1P3
Phone: 416-736-5135
Fax: 416-736-5447
E-mail: ltam@yorku.ca

ENGLAND

Retention Support Officers: Support for Students in Context

Teesside University

The Institution and Its Students

Teesside University is a public UK higher education institution in the northeast of England providing undergraduate and postgraduate programs across six academic schools (faculties). The University has a wide range of programs, a number of which are vocational. The majority of students are from the region and commute, although about 7% are residential students, living in University halls or University-managed houses. The University has more than 24,000 students, of which 45% are full-time. Nearly 60% of Teesside students are female. Approximately 35% of full-time students are mature (i.e., over age 21), with 91% of part-time students falling into this category. Approximately 6% are from ethnic minorities and about 5% have declared a disability. Teesside has a strong commitment to widening participation, and about 40% of its students are from lower socioeconomic groups. Overall, more than half of the students at Teesside can be defined as first-generation.

The Initiative

When we researched the experience of first-year students at Teesside in 2004-2005 (University of Teesside Retention Team, 2005), we discovered that many students felt very supported at the institution, but many also felt they did not want to bother a member of **academic staff** with small questions (e.g., understanding what a seminar is, where classes are held, what a particular type of **assessment** is, where to go to get help with financial problems, who to contact if you have missed a deadline, what to do if you miss classes due to illness, how you get help if you are having problems with writing or math). However, it became obvious that these small questions were often fundamental to students' retention and success. While the University provides excellent help for all of these issues, it was noted that first-generation, first-year students often do not know how to access such assistance.

The Retention Support Officers (RSOs) initiative was developed to provide context-specific support for students. RSOs are school-based support staff who provide first-year students with a bridge to the range of support mechanisms available both within the academic schools and across the University. They also assist course teams and teaching staff in developing and implementing appropriate retention strategies. The RSOs' involvement in each school is designed to suit the particular needs of the discipline areas in that school, but all of the RSOs also act as a bridge between the student and the institution. A critical RSO role is to provide students with easy access to answers to questions students may deem dumb, but which may have a seriously negative effect on the quality of their university experience if left unanswered.

Specifically, the RSOs provide nonacademic, face-to-face drop-in support for students, particularly those in their first year. In addition, they undertake supportive attendance monitoring, which involves contacting students who have missed classes to ask if they have any problems and helping them re-engage and/or get more specific help. The RSOs also facilitate peer support for students and evaluate school-based retention data.

This initiative has been in place since October 2005 and continues to be enhanced annually. An important factor to the success of the initiative is that each school has an RSO who is based in its buildings but who is line-managed jointly by the school dean of learning and teaching and by the central head of student retention. This ensures that the RSO is providing the types of support appropriate to the specific context and needs of each school and enables a strategic institutional overview of both the activities of the RSOs and retention issues for the whole institution. Good practice in each school is shared across the University through fortnightly meetings of the team of six RSOs with the head of the Student Retention Team. RSOs also participate in joint staff development activities to ensure students from every area of the University receive the best support, advice, and learning experiences. The RSOs are visible, friendly, approachable, and can refer any student in need to the appropriate resource. A key factor in the success and effectiveness of this initiative is that what is best for each student is the priority rather than retention rates or the concerns of a school or a particular **course** or program.

Research Design

Since the development of this initiative, it has been evaluated in a variety of ways. The introduction of RSOs followed a major two-year research project in 2003-2005 at the University funded by the European Social Fund (ESF), a funding body that directs research and implementation funding to projects that support a range of disadvantaged groups, often within education. The success of the research project led to a follow-up project funded by ESF during 2005-2007, which focused on the implementation of the strategies identified in the original research project, including the introduction of the RSOs. Student feedback has been elicited through questionnaires from 200 nontraditional students who had all accessed the RSOs as part of the implementation project. Student focus groups have also been used to explore the role of the RSOs and other retention initiatives. In addition, analysis was undertaken of the individual feedback forms completed anonymously by students after they received assistance from an RSO. Academic staff were also asked for their views on the role of the RSO.

To track the overall impact on retention rates, statistical data on student retention and progression have also been monitored over the three years that the initiative has been in place. However, it is important to note that the RSO initiative is one of several retention initiatives introduced during that time period. Therefore, it is difficult to differentiate the specific impact of this role.

Research Findings

Retention has improved annually. The withdrawal rate in 2005 was 21% but has steadily declined since the implementation of RSOs (18.5% in 2006, 15.5% in 2007, and 14.6% in 2008). This improvement exceeded expectations from the national funding body, which establishes national benchmarks for each individual university based upon its student profile and portfolio of courses. Teesside's performance has exceeded its benchmark and national trends for modern (post-1993) universities in the UK.

There has been a range of positive feedback from students about the RSOs and the help they provide, as evidenced by one student's comment, "It was really good to talk to someone who I felt I could ask anything." Students also provided feedback on the bridging aspects of the role:

> I was grateful to the RSO for helping to set up meetings with the student mentors. I now feel more comfortable with the subject.

> It was good to have a friendly face to talk to and someone who could initiate contact with a member of staff.

In addition, teaching staff have indicated the RSOs have made their job easier:

> I'd like to say that having ... a retention officer has really begun to make a difference to the program in terms of attendance. Many of our students who were poor attenders in the first few weeks are now attending regularly. Also feedback from students is that they really appreciate having an approachable, friendly, and helpful person who they can go to if they're having problems.

Perhaps the main difficulty we have had with the role is educating people to its uniqueness. Some staff view the role as an administrative one, and it is sometimes challenging to ensure that the activities of the RSO in some schools continues to be outreach-based and interactive, rather than focused on the administrative aspects of monitoring attendance. However, the particular strengths of the role seem to lie in this same uniqueness in the cooperation among the individual RSOs. The post was piloted in 2004 in one school and was successful, but its effectiveness has increased exponentially since there has been a retention support officer in all schools. RSOs work in their particular school context, but they also work together by sharing good practice, ideas, and coordinating their efforts through the central Student Retention Team.

Implications

The role of retention support officer is now well established in the University and is an integrated aspect of the overall retention approach of the institution and a valued aspect of student support. The deputy vice chancellor meets annually with the RSOs to talk with them about issues for students in the **faculties**. Other universities and colleges have begun exploring how they can adapt the idea in their own contexts. We would argue that there are important factors that make this strategy as successful as it is and that need to be considered by other institutions wishing to introduce similar approaches.

First, the RSOs are based in the faculty, which makes them both more accessible for students and recognizable to teachers. Second, their priority is the students. The RSOs from each faculty work together as a team across faculties and are jointly line-managed by a faculty-based manager and the head of the central retention team, providing an important cross-university overview to the role. It is possible to have an RSO in only one faculty, and that was how we started; however, the impact on student retention is far greater with a team of support officers working together, and individually, to support students in their faculty context and across the whole University.

References

The University of Teesside Retention Team. (2005). *Retaining non-traditional students in higher education*. Middlesbrough: University of Teesside.

Contributors

Diane Nutt
Head of the Student Retention Team
Centre for Learning and Quality Enhancement
University of Teesside
Middlesbrough
Tees Valley
TS1 3BA
Phone: +44 (0) 1642 342541
E-mail: diane.nutt@tees.ac.uk

Lesley Greer
Learning and Teaching Fellow

ENGLAND

Peer-Assisted Study Sessions: Personalizing the Learning Experience

The University of Manchester

The Institution and Its Students

The University of Manchester is the largest single-site higher education institution in the United Kingdom, with more than 35,000 students studying a wider variety of academic subjects than any other UK university. It is a research-intensive public university and was named University of the Year in the *Times Higher Education Supplement* in 2005 and by the *Sunday Times* in 2006. The number of undergraduate full-time students totals 26,460 (46.5% male, 53.3% female), 91.7% of **first-degree entrants** were under 21 on entry. The University offers more than 9,200 residential places, almost all of which are within two to three miles of the campus.

Home to around 7,000 overseas students from more than 150 countries, the University is a multicultural environment. The racial/ethnic background of undergraduate students is 78.4% White, 9.1% South Asian (i.e., Bangladeshi, Indian, Pakistani), 1.7% Chinese, 1.0% other Asian background, 2.5% Black (i.e., African, Caribbean, other), and 3.3% other (including mixed race). Race/ethnicity data are not available for 4% of the undergraduate population.

The Initiative

Peer support was first introduced into the University in 1995. Two distinct, yet complementary schemes exist within the institution: Peer Mentoring and Peer-Assisted Study Sessions (PASS). Peer Mentoring is a social network focusing primarily on nonacademic support, assisting with orientation, socialization, and ongoing transition. Peer mentors are encouraged to develop proactive intervention strategies throughout the course of the year in addition to responding to individual student inquiries. There are currently in excess of 1,500 mentors operating in more than 35 disciplines.

Both Mentoring and PASS seek to enhance the student experience through developing a supportive environment to assist transition. This case will focus on the aims and objectives of PASS and the evidenced student benefit.

PASS derives from the American Supplemental Instruction (SI) model developed at the University of Missouri, Kansas City (UMKC) in 1973 by Deana Martin (Arendale, 1994). Supplemental Instruction (SI) is a peer-facilitated academic assistance program that targets historically difficult courses so as to improve student performance and retention by offering regularly scheduled, informal review sessions. Students learn how to integrate course content and study skills while working together.

In the early 1990s, Jenni Wallace (working at Kingston University) adapted the SI model for use in British higher education and in doing so developed, in consultation with other institutions, the "21 Principles of SI" (The University of Manchester, 2007). At Manchester, it is recognized that "Two essential features of SI are that it is voluntary, and that it is not seen as remedial in nature so that able students participate to the benefit of all" (Coe, McDougall, & McKeown, 1999, *p*. 72).

PASS utilizes the experience and expertise of higher-year students (PASS leaders) by training them as facilitators, not teachers or tutors, to support their group of lower-year students in finding solutions to problems and understanding complex concepts through facilitated discussion and guided questioning. Each group's pair of PASS leaders encourage active learning in an informal, friendly, and fun environment that does not seek to replace the interaction between **staff** and student. Rather, PASS provides another opportunity for students to enter into institutional discourse with their peers (Harvey, Drew, & Smith, 2006). Each discipline takes responsibility for their scheme by identifying at least three coordinators (academic; administrative; and a student, who is an experienced PASS leader). These key posts work with specialist staff in the University's central Teaching and Learning Support Office to maintain and develop the scheme. The central coordination and advice assures and enhances the quality of Manchester's scheme and, therefore, its recognition as the national benchmark for PASS/SI schemes.

PASS at Manchester aims to:

◇ Support student learning by encouraging collaborative, exploratory discussion in a safe environment
◇ Enhance the learning experience and personal development of PASS leaders
◇ Improve academic performance and achievement and increase retention
◇ Provide an additional mechanism for communication and feedback between teaching staff and students
◇ Encourage a student-centered approach to learning through greater peer interaction

The culmination of these aims is surmised as (a) establishing a supportive environment, (b) enabling deeper conceptual understanding of fundamental academic principles, and (c) increasing individual confidence rather than superficial strategic learning to pass exams.

PASS leaders undergo extensive and ongoing training from staff who are themselves trained as SI supervisors by the International Center for Supplemental Instruction at UMKC[1] to ensure the standard is maintained and that, as leaders, they receive consistent training of a benchmarked quality.

All students from the discipline and modules in which PASS operates are eligible to attend the weekly, **timetabled** sessions regardless of their academic ability. In the academic year 2007-2008, PASS was operating in 14 disciplines[2] (in every **faculty**) with over 350 PASS leaders, making the provision available to more than 2,000 lower-year students.

Research Design

A coordinated, comprehensive evaluation framework crossing all schemes within the University has evolved. Flexibility within the PASS evaluation framework allows disciplines to undertake evaluative research relevant to their own requirements and related to their goals for introducing the scheme. Research is undertaken as collaboration between academic expertise within a discipline and recognized international and national SI/PASS expertise at an institutional level. For the purpose of this chapter, the research questions and findings from the Faculty of Life Sciences are reported to illustrate the generic framework and benefits of PASS. Thus, this chapter considers two research questions:

- Does regular attendance at PASS have an impact on first-year academic performance?
- What do first-years perceive to be the benefits of attending PASS?

The Faculty of Life Sciences (FLS) implemented PASS in 2005-2006, offering it to its first-year cohort (480 students) but split over two semesters (Fostier & Carey, 2007). As such, an experimental control group was identified: those students not offered PASS in Semester 1. One particularly challenging **module**, "Genes and Evolution" (BL1521), was selected as the main focus of discussions in PASS. It is on this module that all students' academic performance is presented and correlated against attendance at PASS, which was collected by **registers** distributed at each session. A questionnaire was also circulated to all first-years to collect qualitative data on their experiences of PASS. Three groups were identified for analysis: (a) students to whom PASS was not offered (Group 1, $n = 158$), (b) students who attended fewer than four PASS sessions (Group 2, $n = 178$), and (c) regular attendees at PASS sessions (Group 3, $n = 54$). It should be noted that Group 1 serves as a control group.

Findings

The main indicator of academic performance is a student's exam result, which is correlated against their attendance at PASS. Donelan and Kay (1998) and Coe et al. (1999) both showed that for students to benefit from PASS their attendance needs to be regular (i.e., attendance at 40-50% of the sessions in either a continuous or discontinuous fashion). In Semester 1, of the 232 students who were offered PASS, 23% were regular attendees (i.e., more than four sessions), which is considered a good participation rate in many schemes (Ashwin, 2003) and exceptional given the scheme was in its pilot year (Ashwin, 2002).

The academic performance of all three groups is presented in Figure 1. A t-test confirms that Groups 1 (i.e., students to whom PASS was not offered) and 2 (i.e., irregular attendees) performed similarly and that their mean **marks** were not significantly different ($p > 0.05$). Those who attended PASS regularly (Group 3) showed an improvement in three key areas:

- They achieved significantly higher mean marks than those in Group 1 (53% vs. 42%, $p < 0.001$) and those in Group 2 (53% vs. 45%, $p < 0.01$).
- They were two times less likely to fail than students who attended PASS irregularly or who were not offered the intervention (22% in Group 3 compared to 42% for Group 2, and 47% for Group 1).
- They were three times more likely to earn first class marks (>70%) than nonattendees (22% vs. 6%) or irregular attendees (22% vs. 7%).

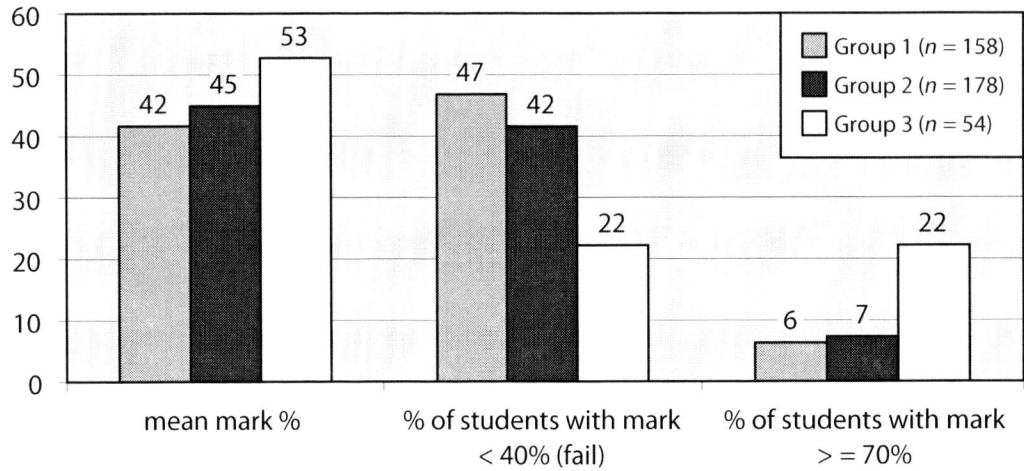

Figure 1. Differences in mean mark for BL1521 in January 2006 by PASS attendance.

It was also reassuring to note that the distribution of students' marks (Figure 2) highlighted the diverse range of academic abilities of those attending, which suggests there was no perceived bias by the student population that PASS was for the gifted or, equally, the remedial student. Figure 2 also shows a positively skewed distribution (toward higher marks) for Group 3 which, when compared with the bell-shaped distribution of the two other groups, suggests regular attendance at PASS could boost a student's mark by 10-20%. Readers will find it interesting that these data correlate to research undertaken during the early implementation of PASS at Manchester, indicating that regular attendance can increase academic performance by at least one degree classification (Coe et al., 1999)

In terms of the perceived benefits by first-years, the most pleasing (and in some ways surprising) result related to 70% of students identifying "understanding course content" as a key benefit, compared to 40% identifying "preparation for **assessment**" as a benefit. This implies that PASS had "engaged students successfully in a meaning gathering approach rather than a purely strategic one" (Fostier & Carey, 2007, p. 148). Students also identified the social and study skills benefits of PASS, recognizing "adjusting to University/pastoral care" and "developing study and transferable skills" as important elements of each session (Fostier, Speake, & Sheffield, 2006).

PASS leaders identified similar benefits for first-years, but they also recognized benefits for themselves. In particular, they noted benefits such as increased academic performance (Garside, Embury, & Carey, 2006), transferable skills, and a deeper approach to learning (Donelan & Kay, 1998)—all of which have previously been documented. In addition to researching the benefits to the recipients of the support, there is perhaps a need to place a greater emphasis on researching and reporting the benefits to the PASS leaders who commit time, effort, and enthusiasm (often voluntarily) to enhance the student experience.

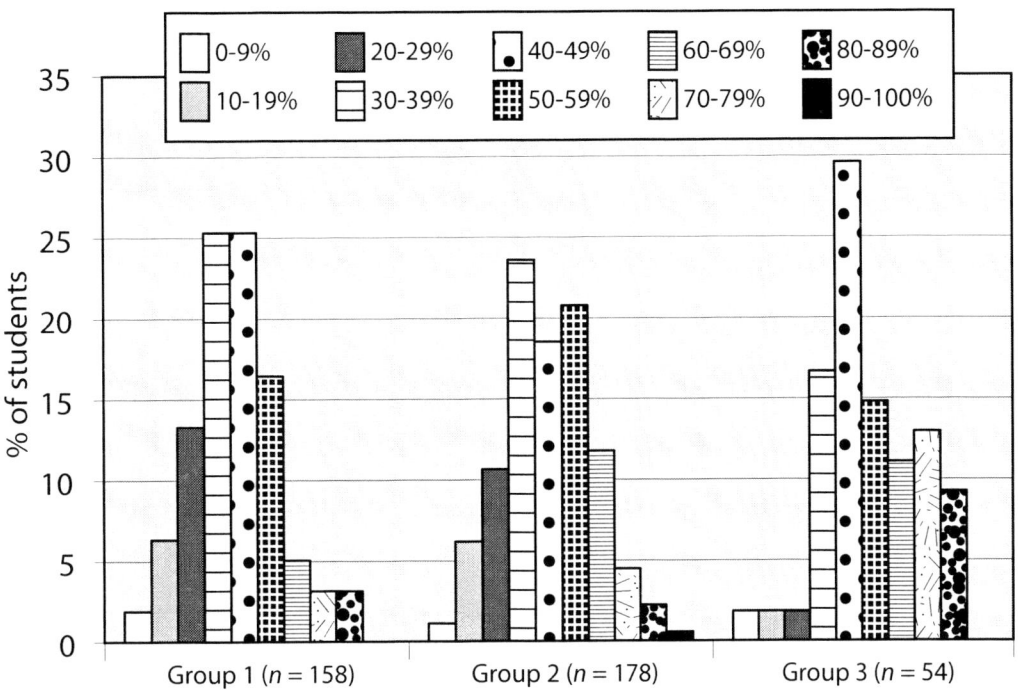

Figure 2. Mark distributions for BL1521 by PASS attendance.

Implications

To date all research carried out within The University of Manchester supports the national and international findings of significant benefits to regular attendees. The University of Manchester recognizes the value of PASS and the benefits it provides to the numerous internal and external stakeholders in addition to regular attendees.

PASS is embedded within the institution's Students as Partners program and is recognized as good practice in supporting and enhancing the Manchester student experience. As with many pedagogic approaches to developing the independent learner, PASS at The University of Manchester has evolved (within the parameters of the international SI principles) through the understanding of practical implications and the development of processes for implementation and expansion. The benefits of introducing PASS are significant, but the development and pilot phases of PASS require significant investment, commitment, and enthusiasm. As such, practitioners seeking to implement SI or PASS would be wise not to reinvent the wheel but instead to utilize the wealth of knowledge, expertise, and lessons learned available through an international network. Practice, resources, and research are collated and disseminated through National Centres, who work in partnership with the International Center for Supplemental Instruction to provide consultancy to individual institutions and disciplines.

PASS as a model promotes engagement and partnership of staff and students. The University of Manchester has benefited from staff and student enthusiasm, which has driven the strategic expansion and enhancement of PASS. Internally, this enthusiasm (both operationally and strategically) is indicative of the wiser, external SI/PASS community that actively supports collaboration and creative development.

Notes

[1] The International Center for Supplemental Instruction is based at the University of Missouri, Kansas City (UMKC): www.umkc.edu/cad/si

[2] Disciplines operating PASS are: Mechanical Engineering, Mathematics, Computer Science, Physics, Aerospace Engineering, Life Sciences, Chemistry, Civil Engineering, Chemical Engineering, Materials Science, Economics, Music, Middle Eastern Studies, and Psychology

References

Arendale, D. (1994). Understanding the supplemental instruction model. In D. Martin & D. Arendale (Eds.), *Supplemental instruction: Increasing achievement and retention* (New Directions for Teaching and Learning, No 60, pp. 11-21). San Francisco: Jossey-Bass.

Ashwin, P. (2002). Implementing peer learning across organisations: The development of a model. *Mentoring and Tutoring, 10*(3), 221-231.

Ashwin, P. (2003). Peer support: Relations between the context, process and outcomes for students who are supported. *Instructional Science, 31*, 159-173.

Coe, E., McDougall, A., & McKeown, N. (1999). Is peer assisted learning of benefit to undergraduate chemists? *University Chemistry Education, 3*(2), 72-75.

Donelan, M., & Kay, P. (1998). Supplemental instruction: Students helping students' learning at University College London (UCL) and University of Central Lancashire (UCLAN). *The International Journal of Legal Education, 32*(3), 287-299.

Fostier, M., & Carey, W. (2007). *Exploration, experience and evaluation: Peer Assisted Study Scheme (PASS), sharing the experience of The University of Manchester: 480 1st year bioscience students.* Paper presented at the Science, Learning, and Teaching Conference, Keele University, UK.

Fostier, M., Speake, T., & Sheffield, L. (2006, May). *Evaluation of the implementation of Peer Assisted Study Sessions (PASS) on a major scale for Biosciences 1st year undergraduates at Manchester University (UK).* Paper presented at the Supplemental Instruction International Conference, Malmo, Sweden.

Garside, J., Embury, S., & Carey, W. (2006, May). *Changing the student, changing the culture.* Paper presented at the Supplemental Instruction International Conference, Malmo, Sweden.

Harvey, L., Drew, S., & Smith, M. (2006). *The first-year experience: A review of literature for the Higher Education Academy.* York: Higher Education Academy.

The University of Manchester. (2007). *PASS at The University of Manchester*. Retrieved September 26, 2007, from http://www.campus.manchester.ac.uk/tlso/studentsaspartners/peersupport/pass

Contributors

Marcia Ody
Teaching and Learning Manager
The University of Manchester
Oxford Road,
Manchester
M13 9PL
Phone: 0161 275 3254
E-mail: marcia.ody@manchester.ac.uk

William Carey
Teaching and Learning Adviser (Students as Partners)
E-mail: william.carey@manchester.ac.uk

ENGLAND

Exploring the Use of E-portfolios and Blogs to Support the Transition Into Higher Education for Foundation Degree Students

University of Wolverhampton

The Institution and Its Students

The University of Wolverhampton, located in the West Midlands of the United Kingdom, is a public-controlled institution that offers primarily three- and four-year undergraduate **courses** and postgraduate study up to and including doctoral programs. It has 10 academic schools covering a broad range of subjects. The University is based on four campuses in Wolverhampton, Walsall, and Telford. Three of the campuses have residential **accommodations**, but a large proportion of students are from the local area.

In 2005-2006, the University had 23,560 students: 59% full-time, 41% part-time, and 41.5% over 25 years of age. Nearly 60% of students were female, 32.1% represented an ethnic minority group, and 3.8% of students declared a disability.

The Initiative

Expanding student numbers, improved access by learners from nontraditional backgrounds, and consumer-centric expectations of a high-quality learning experience have combined to symbolically and literally change the higher education landscape and challenge existing relationships between institutions and their students. Driven by unease about students' preparation for employment, apprehension over retention performance indicators, and concerns about how students are supported throughout their academic lives, the national Quality Assurance Agency of England and Wales (QAA) promoted progress files (PF) and personal development planning (PDP) to help students "reflect upon their own learning and achievements and to plan for their own personal, educational, and career development" (QAA, 2001, p.12).

The University of Wolverhampton's response to the above agenda was to design and adopt an electronic portfolio system, PebblePAD (www.pebblelearning.co.uk), which was made available to all **staff** and students in September 2005. The initiative described here built upon two years of e-portfolio use by practitioners and sought to examine the outcomes associated with the use of educational weblogs (blogs) with a group of foundation degree students. Foundation degrees, aimed at vocational student groups less traditionally associated with higher education, were established in England in 2000 in response to "a context of growing dissatisfaction with the existing vocational provision at HE level" (Reeve, Gallacher, & Ingram, 2007, p. 307). This "earn and learn" approach allows students to access subdegree qualifications in a flexible manner, usually around their full-time work commitments. In particular, we wanted to study whether the use of blogs as a dialogic pedagogical tool supported the transition into higher education, built confidence and self-esteem, and created a sense of belonging in a group of 30 part-time female foundation degree students studying at the University in 2006-2007. All students worked in regional primary and secondary education settings as teaching assistants (TAs) and learning mentors. These students were not net-generation learners or digital natives.

The students attended University for two evenings per week. Individual reflective blogging, with writing prompts, was introduced from **induction** as both an ice-breaker and a PDP tool to support the development of reflective thinking and writing. By emphasizing narratives, we encouraged students to tell their learning autobiographies and continuing learning stories in their own words and at their own pace. Rapid and supportive tutor feedback was a key feature. Writing frames/scaffolds were offered to support the weekly writing activities as we were aware that for many new students writing in an academic context was a feared activity. We wanted to emphasize that informal blog writing was a practice or warm-up for the more formal academic writing to follow.

Once individual blogging confidence had developed, collaborative blogging activities were introduced in an attempt to deepen and support the emergent face-to-face community of practice (Lave & Wenger, 1991) and to promote critical reflection upon their status as "becoming" higher education students. By adopting and adapting the problem-based approach used in the face-to-face classroom, we created structured blog posts that required the group to share their perceptions, experiences, and reflections upon subjects such as "what is academic writing?". No formal guidelines on content or posting frequency were established other than respecting the negotiated ground rules of our learning spaces.

Research Design

All 30 students shared individual reflective blogs with the course tutors and engaged in the community blog. Both sets of blogs were considered as data following a method termed *interview plus*, where the plus represents some artifact or activity chosen to guide recall or aid thinking aloud (Mayes, 2006). The research method also used individual questionnaires, focus groups, and semi-structured interviews, which were analyzed using an interpretative phenomenological approach as described by Reid, Flowers, and Larkin (2005, cited in Creanor, Trinder, Gowan, & Howells, 2006). This methodology is premised upon the idea that the interviewee is an expert on their own experiences.

The dialogic approach to data gathering focused on online discussions, reflections, and the artifacts created by students, which went on to stimulate further reflections in their summative essays. This approach allowed issues and themes to be validated, explored, and developed both with individuals and within groups using the e-portfolio space like an online interview or focus group.

Findings

The data suggest that the use of individual and community blogs was a key factor in the confidence that grew in this emergent community of practice and that blogs facilitated a positive transition into higher education for these students. When asked to characterize in three words how they felt during the first three weeks of University, students' responses were overwhelmingly negative: "sick," "nervous," "no self-confidence," "thick," "confused," "overwhelmed," and "lost." When asked to reflect on the use of blogs in the transition into higher education, student responses were more positive as evidenced by these statements:

> I feel it supported my learning greatly. Due to being dyslexic, I found the writing frames fantastic!

> Pebble Pad is a wonderful support facility for students. Initially I was dubious—never having done anything like this before—but as a communication tool I found it fun and (amazingly!) easy to use. The support that being in touch with others gives is a great motivational tool.

> As an H.E student, my confidence grew tremendously because I had no idea what I was letting myself in for initially! Found that I really enjoyed the challenge and stimulation of university life. My experience at Uni has strengthened my belief in myself at work. I am much more confident and happy to try out new strategies with children.

The blog allowed for rapid tutor and peer feedback, encouragement, and support early in the transition when student confidence was particularly low, and this contributed to the students' experiencing a sense of belonging in their new life in higher education:

> I felt it was a good way to communicate and share our concerns and worries. To be able to log reflections was very useful when writing study skills assignments. I have also been able to use these reflections in other modules. Also it's great to read back and think, "Did that really worry me?"

However, not all students were convinced of the usefulness of the blogging. Three of 30 students felt that neither the individual or community blog activity had any relevance to them or their development. As outlined in Wang, Fix, and Bock (2004), not all blogs are successful and not all students want to take part in "conversations beyond the classroom." It is important to acknowledge that for some this is a more painful transition. As one student noted, "I did not enjoy this exercise, would have preferred to type stuff up in Word, which is what I can relate to." Blogging may also create inequalities, as this comment from another student suggests: "I felt out of the loop when I didn't have time to blog with members of the group."

Despite this dissatisfaction with blogging from a small group of students, half of the foundation degree students in the program attributed improvement in their reflective writing to their use of the blogs and the writing spaces and the practice opportunities they facilitated. They felt this contributed to their good grades. Compared to similar foundation degree groups who did not use the e-portfolio, there were 50% more A-C grades for the first semester assignment than in the previous year. Ultimately, the research showed that it was the grade and the feedback from the paper-based summative assignment that gave students the greatest confidence boost, and perhaps a sense of belonging in higher education.

> I have achieved so much this year personally, and my confidence had completely grown and the fact that my assignments were coming back with fantastic **marks** was a real spur, so much so, that I entered a writing competition, which I won—Lucia Terry, Foundation degree student, 2007.

When asked to reflect in three words upon how they felt at the end of their first year, "confident," "happy," and "assertive" were common responses along with "exhausted" and "relieved."

The community of practice supported the development of key relationships, and the community (real and virtual) continued to grow in strength even when blog activity slowed down, suggesting that the program also supported students' social adjustment to higher education. As one student commented, "It was a great way to get to know others that I had not really gotten to know yet. Also sharing our fears and high moments really helped when I hit low times."

Interestingly, the blog continued with about 70% participation throughout the module, and about 35% participation after the module finished for the remainder of the year. When conducting interviews and questionnaires three months after the module had finished, every student said she had checked the blog to see what was happening even though she may not have made a comment on it. "Not having enough time" was a repeated response as to why they were unable to continue their blogging activity.

The transition into higher education can often be painful and difficult. Blogs may provide a supportive platform for students to explore and share feelings about their journey as learners. Blogging offered a way of recording their feelings about their experiences and a forum to discuss these experiences with their peers. Students found their online voices (Oravec, 2002) were often more multidimensional and confident than their classroom voices, giving them the opportunity to become more critically analytical in their thinking. Identifying these online voices and personalities enabled many students to feel more comfortable with the transition to higher education. An online educational blog was not the only reason for this group of students to grow in confidence, but undoubtedly it was a key factor in supporting and encouraging this development and the community of practice that evolved.

Implications and Future Directions

During the earlier two iterations of the foundation degree program, the use of the e-portfolio had not been directly tied to the content. Previously, it was a voluntary activity in addition to the requirements of the course. We learned that the blog was an important space for students to unpack and discuss the module and make sense of their experiences. Many of the conversations and activities on the blog underpinned the content of their assignment and were directly relevant to their studies. Therefore, it was key that this space was integrated into the curriculum and more fully into our learning and teaching strategies. In fact, one lesson learned from this research is that the blog used for academic purposes, rather than as an informal chat space, was more highly rated and valued by this group of foundation degree students. After the initial socialization had taken place, students were concerned with the potential for knowledge development from the blog.

Across the curriculum team, an enthusiasm for using technology to enhance learning was growing, and our successes with blogging encouraged discussions, which led to the revalidation of the foundation degree(s) in a blended format. This approach included taking staff on a technology retreat, which focused on developing the skills and pedagogies for embedding the e-portfolio system within the program rather than viewing it as an add on. We do, however, understand that not all staff are used to the online dialogic approach required for blogging and recognize that some will need support (initial and ongoing) in becoming e-mentors. We also discovered that students felt that it would be beneficial to blog with the previous cohort about their experiences. Because of this, we decided that for the next iteration we would invite peers from a previous cohort to become "blog buddies" and support the new students as e-mentors. No two cohort blogging experiences are the same, for staff or students. It is this fluidity and inability to predict exactly what will happen next year that makes blogging such an exciting learning activity.

References

Creanor, L., Trinder, K., Gowan, D., & Howells, C. (2006). *LEX. The learner experience of e-learning.* Retrieved September 25, 2006, from http://www.jisc.ac.uk/uploaded_documents/LEX%20Final%20Report_August06.pdf

Lave, J., & Wenger, E. (1991). *Situated learning: Legitimate peripheral participation.* Cambridge: University of Cambridge Press.

Mayes, T. (2006). *LEX: Methodology report.* Retrieved September 25, 2006, from http://www.jisc.ac.uk/media/documents/programmes/elearning_pedagogy/lex_method_final.doc

Oravec, J. (2002). Bookmarking the world: Weblog applications in education. *Journal of Adolescent and Adult Literacy, 45*(7), 616-621.

Quality Assurance Agency (QAA). (2001). *Guidelines for HE progress files.* Retrieved August 23, 2005, from http://www.qaa.ac.uk/academicinfrastructure/progressFiles/guidelines/progfile2001.asp

Reeve, F., Gallacher, J., & Ingram, R. (2007). A comparative study of work-based learning within higher nationals in Scotland and foundation degrees in England: Contrast, complexity, and continuity. *Journal of Education and Work, 20*(4), 305-318.

Wang, M., Fix, R., & Bock, L. (2004, October). *Blogs: Useful tool or vain indulgence?* Paper presented at ELearn: 2005 World conference on ELearning in Corporate, Government, Healthcare and Higher Education, Chesapeake, Virginia, USA.

Contributors

Emma Purnell
Researcher
E-mail: j.hughes2@wlv.ac.uk

Julie Hughes
Principal Lecturer
The Institute for Learning Enhancement
The University of Wolverhampton
Wulfruna Street
Wolverhampton
West Midlands WV1 1SB
United Kingdom
Phone: + 44 1902 322361
E-mail: E.purnell@wlv.ac.uk

Developing Peer-Support Skills in Students

Kansai University

The Institution and Its Students

Kansai University (KU), founded in 1886, is one of Japan's most distinguished universities. The University is located in Osaka, the central hub of industry and commerce in Japan. KU currently has 10 faculties and four institutes. KU has approximately 27,000 undergraduate and 2,000 graduate students from all over Japan.

The two educational philosophies of KU are to harmonize theory and practice and to acknowledge the importance of internationalization. KU has been making great efforts to deepen international understanding and encourages students to have an independent spirit, develop their character, and expand their knowledge. As a result, KU is regarded as a "university that fosters human resources matching social demands." KU hopes to encourage prosocial attitudes and behaviors in its graduates.

To act on these educational ideals, KU supports not only students' curricular activities but also extracurricular activities such as the Athletic Association, Extracurricular Study Association, and various volunteer activities. There are more than 300 clubs at KU, and nearly half (55.2%) of the students belong to at least one club. However, only 12.2% students have taken part in volunteer activities. The initiative described below was designed to help students make a successful transition to the university but also to foster empathy and prosocial (i.e., altruistic) attitudes, which make participation in volunteer activities and civic life more likely.

The Initiative

In response to the lack of independence and poor communication skills seen among college students in recent years, KU instituted the peer-community program as a means to address these concerns. This program also supports the transition of foreign students and first-year students to KU, who are likely to need the most help in establishing a comfortable life on campus. Students come to acquire the ability to think and act creatively and independently by relating to peers in this community. It is also believed that through building peer relationships, students will develop greater empathy and come to hold more prosocial attitudes.

The peer community is an independent group managed by student volunteers who are interested in supporting every aspect of a first-year student's campus life. For example, the KU Bridge Community aims to provide support for international students. Student volunteers have hosted calligraphy lessons, picked students up at the airport, offered practice in Japanese conversation, and helped with term papers. These activities were well-received by international students.

The peer-community program is related to the "all campus revision" enacted at KU in 2008, which included a curricular program to foster skills and knowledge in practical communication and techniques for peer support. In addition to this curricular program, the Office of the Dean of Students also opened a preparatory office for student support and conducts an extracurricular program to facilitate the peer-support community. Both programs have supported the efforts of student volunteers to establish and maintain a consultation counter and to hold campus events. This program offers an informal counseling center where other students can drop in to ask questions about classes or becoming involved on campus and to learn strategies for succeeding in the University.

The preparatory office supports students in obtaining the necessary qualifications to become a peer-support instructor by offering the courses necessary to qualify as an instructor of peer support recognized by The Japan Peer Support Association. The program provides students with opportunities for gaining professional expertise, practicing independent problem solving, and establishing interpersonal boundaries.

As part of their membership in the peer community program, first-year students attend a series of 12 sessions in a peer-support class designed to highlight three themes: (a) understanding KU and the student's place within it, Theme 1; (b) developing communication skills, Theme 2; and (c) developing problem-solving skills, Theme 3. Table 1 provides the 12 session topics and their connection to these themes. The peer-support class is led by professors together with qualified peer-support instructors. The class is an important part of the peer-community program, and it is open to all first-year students on the campus.

Table 1

Content of the Peer-Support Class

Instruction Type	Topic	Theme
	1. Orientation	
Lecture	2. Raise your awareness as college students	1
Lecture	3. Enhance your sense of belonging as a student at KU	1
Lecture	4. Design your campus life	1
Practice	5. Develop your communication skills	2
Lecture	6. Think about the relationship between mind and body	2
Practice	7. Manage your emotions by moving your body	2
Lecture	8. Learn what stress is and how to manage it	3
Lecture	9. Learn the social skills rooted in psychological theory	2
Practice	10. Learn how to listen	2
Lecture	11. Think about communication as problem solving	3
Exam	12. An assessment of the 12 sessions	

Research Design

We measured the effectiveness of peer-support classes by examining changes in three important variables: (a) empathy, (b) prosocial behavior, and (c) prosocial attitudes.

More than 280 students attended the series of lectures, and all students were asked to complete a 42-item **assessment** instrument in April and July (i.e., at the beginning and at the end of the series). Of these, 264 students completed the assessments. First-year students who participated in the peer-support program ($n = 83$, 35 women and 48 men) served as the experimental group (P-Group), while those who did not participate ($n = 181$, 143 women and 48 men) constituted the control group (C-Group). The assessment instrument included three scales:

1. *The Strength of Empathy Scale* (14 items) (Davis, 1983; Sakurai, 1988). In this scale, "perspective-taking" (7 items) and "empathic concern" (7 items) were selected. Statements such as "I want to go easy on an unhappy person" were rated from 4 (strongly agree) to 1 (strongly disagree).
2. *Frequency of Prosocial Behavior* (20 items) (Kikuchi, 1988). Items such as "I raise the fallen child to his feet" were rated from 5 (very frequently) to 1 (never/hardly ever) and measured frequency of altruistic behaviors.
3. *The Strength of Prosocial Attitudes Scale* (15 items) (Hakoi & Takagi, 1987). In this scale, "norm of self-sacrifice" (8 items) and "norm of aiding the weak" (7 items) were measured with items such as, "I (We) should help those ..." These items were rated from 5 (strongly agree) to 1 (strongly disagree).

A two-factor ANOVA (group factor vs. time factor) was used to determine the relationship between participating in the 12 successive lectures and the development of empathy and prosocial attitudes and behaviors. It was assumed that the more students were affected by the successive lectures, the more likely they would be to display empathy and prosocial attitudes and behaviors, which, in turn, would have a positive impact on their communication skills.

Findings

Empathy

As seen from Figure 1, the main effect of time and group interaction of both factors were all statistically significant ($F = 199.07$, $F = 99.85$, $F = 321.79$, $p < .001$). The P-group maintained higher empathy scores compared with C-group, suggesting that participation in the peer community may support the development of empathy.

Prosocial Behavior

The main effect of time was significant ($F = 9.71$, $p < .01$), and the main effect of group suggested the tendency of significance ($F = 3.64$, $p < .10$). However, the interaction of time and group were not significant. According to Figure 2, students of both groups engage in prosocial behavior more frequently in July compared with April. Prosocial behavior appears to increase with time, but this change does not appear to be related to participation in the peer program.

In Japan, high school and junior high school students do not typically engage in prosocial behaviors because they regard these behaviors as *dasai* (i.e., putting on airs or engaging in hypocritical behavior). It is possible that the university environment releases them from this restriction.

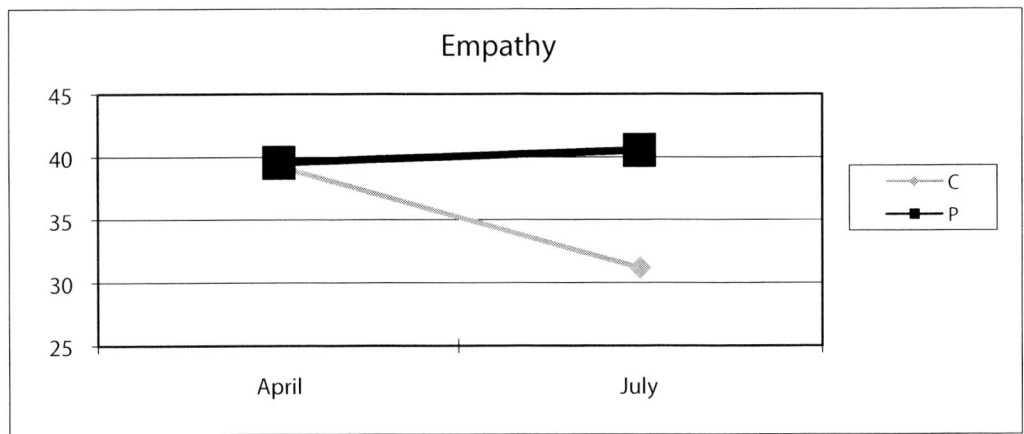

Figure 1. Change in empathy score for participants and nonparticipants.

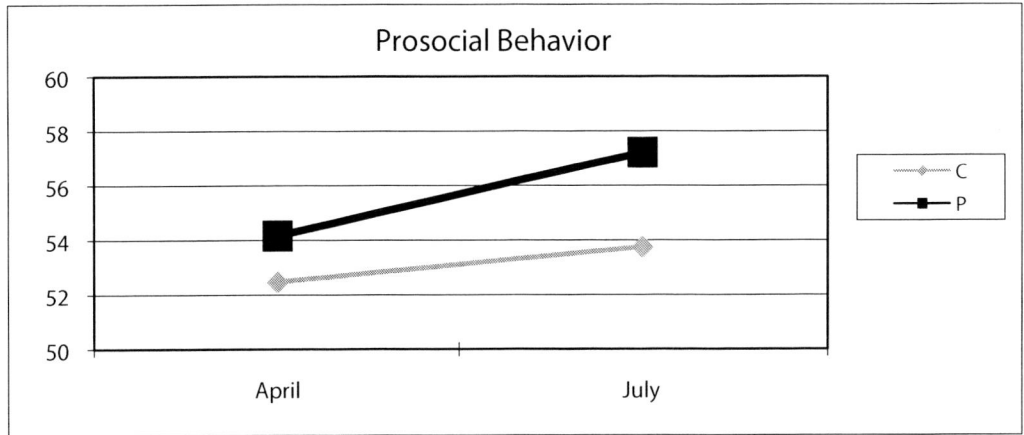

Figure 2. Change in prosocial behavior score for participants and nonparticipants.

Prosocial Attitudes

The adoption of a helping norm is a prerequisite of prosocial behavior. At the same time, such attitudes are likely related to the development of empathy. The main effect of time was significant ($F = 14.05, p < .001$), but the main effect of group was not significant. The interaction of two factors suggested the tendency of significance ($F = 3.51, p < .10$). Prosocial attitudes decreased over time, but that decrease was larger for students within the control group, suggesting that participation in successive lectures may have mediated this change to some extent (Figure 3).

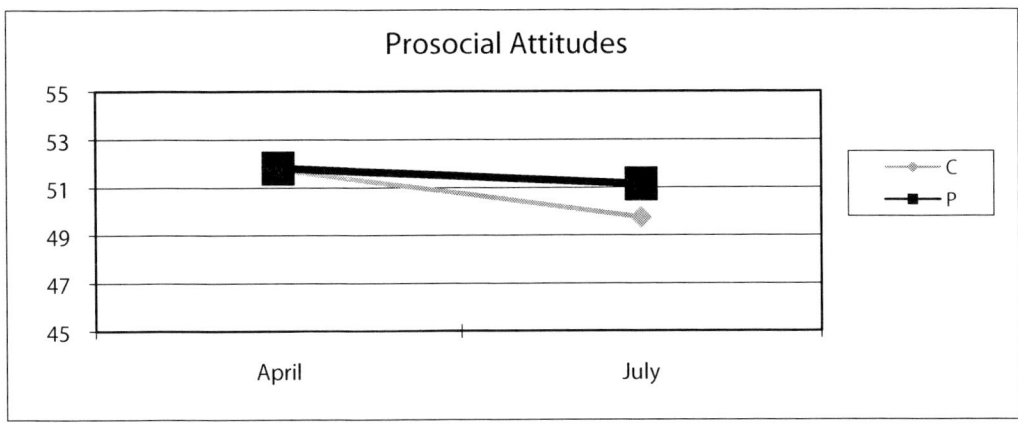

Figure 3. Change in prosocial attitudes for participants and nonparticipants.

Implications

The strength of empathy and awareness of prosocial attitudes have the tendency to decrease if they are left alone. The experience of attending peer-support classes has an effect of maintaining the initial level of these measures.

The frequency of prosocial behavior increases when students enter into the University, a phenomenon seen in both groups. It is suggested that the prosocial behavior of Japanese students, at least in junior high school or high school students, is restricted by their implicit consensus that prosocial or moral behaviors are not acceptable. These inhibitions might be eased when they transitioned into the University community.

The program used here might have contributed greatly to sustaining the level of strength of empathy and prosocial attitudes in Japan.

References

Davis, M. H. (1983). Measuring individual differences in empathy: Evidence for a multidimensional approach. *Journal of Personality and Social Psychology, 44*, 113-126.

Hakoi, H., & Takagi, O. (1987). A comparative study of normative attitude toward helping the different groups of sex, age, and generation. *Journal of Social Psychology, 3*(1), 39-47.

Kikuchi, A. (1988). *Omoiyari wo kagaku suru [Studying the science of sympathy]*. Tokyo: Kawashima-Shoten.

Sakurai, S. (1988). The relationship between empathy and helping behavior in college students. *Journal of Nara University of Education, 37*(1), 149-154.

Contributors

Toshiya Tanaka
Professor of Psychology
Dean of the Graduate School of Psychology
Kansai University
3-3-35, Yamate-cho, Suita City, OSAKA
564-8680 JAPAN
Phone: +81-6-6368-0497
E-mail: ttank@kansai-u.ac.jp

Yoshinori Yamada
Graduate Student of Psychology
E-mail: ra8m512@.kansai-u.ac.jp

Takashi Oshie
Graduate Student of Psychology
E-mail:oshie.is.not.osue@gmail.com

MOROCCO

The First-Year Seminar

Sidi Mohamed Ben Abdallah University

The Institution and Its Students

Sidi Mohamed Ben Abdallah University is a three-year public institution in Fez, Morocco. The initiative described here is housed in the Faculty of Arts and Human Sciences, which enrolled 7,580 full-time undergraduate students in 2006-2007. Of those, 40% (3,032 students) lived on campus. The rest commuted to campus, including some students who live in town outside the campus. Of the students in Arts and Human Sciences, 1,100 are full-time undergraduate students enrolled in the English Modular Degree Programme (Department of English), representing 14.5% of the institution's total student population. Students enrolled in the English Modular Degree Programme (EMDP) are 60% female, and 84% of them are under the age of 25. Approximately 86% of EMDP students are first-generation college students.

The Initiative

Making the transition from high school to university has always proved a daunting task for first-year university students in terms of integration and adaptation to their new academic and social environment. In the context of Moroccan higher education, this problem is reflected in the rates of attrition (up to 70% in some institutions) and the fact that the most vulnerable group are first-year students, as demonstrated by the extremely high rates of dropout among them. Due to the absence of an adequate structure for advising and helping first-year students adapt to their new environment, a great number among them fail to make the transition, which leads to either repeating or dropping out. A first-year seminar (FYS) was developed by the EMDP for students enrolled in the first two semesters of the program. Established in October 2006, the FYS was designed to enhance students' adaptation to their new learning environment and to improve success rates. Specifically, the course sought to

- Help new first-year students achieve a smooth transition from high school to university and become integrated within the environment of the University
- Develop students' ability to make informed choices concerning their selected discipline of study
- Help them to develop the skills necessary for effective learning
- Provide them with information that would enable them to make the most of the challenges and opportunities afforded by university education in terms of self-development and socioeconomic promotion
- Promote their involvement in service and community learning
- Make the students' first year at the University a rewarding and worthwhile experience
- Reduce attrition rates in EMDP, in particular, and across the institution in general

In order to achieve these aims, the course encompasses three main components. First, an information-based component covers topics such as the differences between high school and university, a historical background to the University, selecting a discipline of study at the University, and understanding the organization of EMDP. Second, a skills-based component incorporates in- and out-of-class activities, which include interacting within the university environment, information gathering, time management, making a presentation, and getting involved in and reporting on a community learning experience. Third, a communication-based component involves classroom discussion of a number of local and global issues selected by the students (e.g., the National Initiative for Human Development, immigration, education in Morocco, human rights, the family code, poverty, and terrorism).

Six sections of the FYS, each enrolling 40 students, were offered in academic year 2006-2007. For the academic year 2007-2008, 400 students registered for the course. This case reports on data from the 2006-2007 course.

Research Design

The main aim of the present study was to assess the extent to which the first-year experience of the students involved in the FYS has been positive, especially as it relates to their integration into the university environment. The course was also assessed to determine its impact on attrition rates. Finally, the degree of change in knowledge, skills, and attitudes that contribute to students' academic, cognitive, and social adjustment was measured.

The research procedures assessed the participants' perceived integration into the institution, for example, in the number of new friends they made; their frequency of interaction with other students, faculty, and members of staff; as well as their involvement in extracurricular activities. Data collected from the students' academic records were used to reveal the extent to which they had developed knowledge, skills, and attitudes as a result of their involvement in the FYS.

The evaluation process involved three groups of participants in the implementation of the FYS: (a) the 240 students enrolled in the FYS in 2006-2007, (b) 15 graduate students (peer leaders), and (c) six faculty members who taught the course. It also involved five faculty members who did not teach the FYS but who had been informed about its different stages and the progress of its implementation.

In addition to participant observation by faculty members who taught the FYS, classroom observation was also carried out by faculty members not involved in teaching the course and the peer leaders. Using video recording and note taking, the observers reported on patterns of interaction among students and with teachers and on various aspects of students' behavior during the FYS sessions (e.g., observed preparation for class, frequency and type of participation, types of questions asked, elicitation of teacher feedback).

Semi-structured interviews were also conducted to collect data for the evaluation of the initiative from a sample of 48 students (20% random sample). The interview was designed to elicit information about the following:

- Students' knowledge about the institution prior to enrollment
- Involvement in group work in and outside class
- Degree of adaptation to the academic environment (e.g., understanding of teachers' expectations, time management, class attendance, and preparation for exams)
- Interaction in the classroom (e.g., participation in class, interaction with other students and with teachers)
- Interaction outside class with students, faculty, and staff
- Use of institution services (e.g., library, computer facilities, and health services)
- Involvement in community learning and service activities
- Overall satisfaction with the experience

Further data were collected during a study day (i.e., a day dedicated to FYS program evaluation) attended by the faculty who taught the course, graduate students who acted as peer leaders, 24 students (four representatives from each section), and 15 invited faculty and staff members. During the study day, the student representatives were each invited to make a 10-minute presentation about their evaluation of the FYS, and the invited participants asked them questions and made comments. The study day was video recorded, followed by a transcription and analysis of relevant data on the participants' overall experience, their frequency and quality of interaction with other students and faculty, their involvement in academic and social activities within the institution and outside, and the perceived effect of the FYS on their academic performance.

A statistical survey of the students' academic results as recorded in their grade transcripts was used to assess the potential effect of the FYS on their academic performance.

Findings

Retention and Academic Performance

Prior to the implementation of FYS, as many as 75% of first-year students failed to re-register for the following year and were considered drop outs. As Table 1 indicates, this figure decreased to 17% for EMDP students, with an additional rate of 58% persisters re-registering and, therefore, ensuring a further chance of completing the course. While the importance of this rate of retention as an indicator of future academic success needs further supporting evidence, it does clearly show a drastic decrease in the drop-out rate among the first-year students, unprecedented in our institution.

Table 1

EMDP Retention and Course Completion Rates, 2006-2007 (N = 240)

	N	%
Level 1*(Semester 1)		
Passed	155	64.5
Failed	85	35.5
Level 2* (Semester 2)		
Passed	163	68.0
Failed	77	32.0
Levels 1 & 2		
Passed	145	60.5
Failed	95	39.5
2007-2008		
Failed to register for the course	41	17.0

* The course is organized into two levels, covered consecutively in Semesters 1 and 2.

Student Learning

The in-depth interviews and classroom observations carried out by faculty not involved in teaching the FYS revealed important changes in the students' study habits, their patterns of interaction in the classroom, and their degree of participation. The positive change observed in these three areas was particularly evident in the students' improved time management, their ability to locate and effectively use information necessary for achieving learning tasks, and their increased participation in class.

Classroom observations also revealed important changes in the students' talking time compared to faculty talking time. This was emphasized in the comments made by the observers (faculty not involved in teaching the FYS and graduates students) who explained this pattern of classroom behavior with reference to the collaborative/participative teaching strategies adopted in the FYS, as compared to the traditional lecture practices prevailing in the institution at large. The positive effect of group size (a maximum of 40 students in the FYS sections, compared to groups of up to 100 in the other courses of the EMDP) was one of the main factors that contributed to marked improvement in the students' learning and in their degree of satisfaction with their experience of the FYS initiative.

Interaction With Students and Faculty

Another area in which an important change was noticed was the degree of interaction of students with peers and faculty both inside and outside the classroom. A number of interviewees mentioned with enthusiasm how the first two sessions (on introductions and group forming) provided opportunities for them "to make friends," "to ask and answer questions without [your] English being corrected," and "to talk to other students outside class about matters related to the course or not." Of additional importance was the reference by some students who were involved in the FYS to interacting with teachers in class "in the corridors" and "even in town." This experience was not universal, however, as some students noted a "fear of daring to knock on the door of the professors' office." This suggests that some, although not all, of the students who have been involved in the FYS activities have managed to develop their motivation and ability to interact with their teachers and seek their help on matters relating to their academic and personal problems.

One notable restriction on the new students' demonstrated readiness to get involved with people in their environment is their reluctance to approach members of the administrative staff. This, as some of the faculty who participated in the evaluation of the FYS initiative indicated, is due on the one hand to the often conflict-oriented relationship that prevails between members of the two groups, and on the other hand, to the lack of a structure designed to facilitate such a relationship. This also explains the students' limited involvement in decision-making bodies at the level of the institution.

Community Involvement

As community involvement within the institution has traditionally been considered a form of political engagement, the FYS students understandably view activities outside sporting ones as incompatible with their study purposes and, therefore, tend to shun them.

However, the fact that global issues constitute an essential component of the FYS led the students to demonstrate a marked understanding of the relationship between discussing such issues in class and actually being/becoming involved in the work of local associations and nongovernmental organizations that address issues like disability, illiteracy, poverty, homelessness, and human rights in the local community or at the national level. A survey of the themes selected by the students for their classroom presentations and the number of students who are now active in community work (65, or 27% of the 2006-2007 cohort) attests to the tremendous impact of the FYS on the students' decision to commit part of their time and energy to assisting members of the community in need of such assistance.

Curricular Innovations

As attested by a majority of faculty and graduate students who participated in a study day on the FYS, the initiative has been instrumental in the introduction of these pedagogical innovations in other courses of the EMDP.

- Teaching small groups as compared to the group size normally prevailing in the institution and addressing the training needs of faculty more familiar with lecturing to large classes
- The adoption of a learner-centered approach to teaching other courses in the EMDP, particularly those in which learning in groups was introduced
- The introduction of a more formative system of evaluation including continuous **assessment** and varied assessment procedures (e.g., in-class quizzes, home assignments, reports, presentations), which have been extended to other courses

Implications and Future Directions

The evaluation of the FYS has revealed encouraging positive outcomes that attest to the effectiveness of the initiative and its relevance in a context of higher education where reform has so far led to dissatisfaction among stakeholders, and where the first-year student's observed inability to achieve a successful transition had resulted in appallingly high rates of attrition. However, the evaluation has also demonstrated a number of problems that need to be addressed through the design of a set of strategies, which include:

- Involving the administrative staff in carrying out the objectives of the FYS, as well as in the evaluation of its outcomes
- Fostering further the students' motivation to interact with members of staff and seeking assistance and services available in the institution
- Enlisting the cooperation of officials of the institution in increasing the number of sections with the aim of reducing group size to a more manageable number of students through the recruitment of new teachers
- Ensuring the involvement of other faculty and staff members in teaching the FYS and offering financial incentives to graduate students
- Reviewing the FYS evaluation procedures to include a quantitative component designed to (a) collect and analyze numerical data, (b) ensure improved validity and reliability of the results, and (c) provide the kind of statistical evidence that is likely to convince decision makers at the institutional and national levels to provide the necessary support for the FYS initiative
- Encouraging the design and implementation of action research projects aimed at addressing issues of first-year transition within the framework of research into higher education
- Ensuring adequate dissemination and sustainability of the initiative

Contributor

Mohamed Ouakrime
Professor
Faculty of Arts & Human Sciences Dhar Mehraz
Sidi Mohamed Ben Abdallah University
46/B Résidence Ennouzha
Route Ain Chkef
Fez, Morocco
Phone: + 212 35600141 / +212 66211767
E-mail: ouakmo2004@yahoo.fr

NEW ZEALAND

Holistic Intervention Program for At-risk Students

Auckland University of Technology

The Institution and Its Students

The Auckland University of Technology (AUT) is located in Auckland City, New Zealand. Previously a technical institution, it now has a total population of 23,000 students, 66% studying full-time. Of these students, 41% are male, and 36% are over 25. The ethnic mix is 8% **Maori**, 8% **Pasifika**, 37% European, and 28% **Asian**; 19% are other or undeclared. Nearly 40% of students speak English as a second language.

AUT is largely a commuter campus; however, there are 700 students in residence. There are a number of **courses** available ranging from one-year certificates through doctoral degrees. There are five faculties: (a) Te Ara Poutama, which is the Faculty of Māori Development; (b) Applied Humanities; (c) Health and Environmental Sciences; (d) Business and Design; and (e) Creative Technologies.

All universities within New Zealand receive partial funding from the government; the percentage is set annually and based on a number of criteria. In addition to this, students are required to pay fees, which may be covered through personal financing or the student loan scheme.

The Initiative

This intervention and monitoring strategy is based on a holistic model. It seeks to provide proactive intervention and support to first-year students who are identified as at risk, as determined by student applications (e.g., incomplete applications or selection of programs that are very different from each other), attendance, and **assessments**. Using the University's in-house computer system, students are tracked and monitored over the semester or year. Electronic reports are generated, identifying those students who may be at risk of withdrawing or failing.

These students are then proactively contacted by telephone and offered support. Senior student mentors, who undergo rigorous training and are paid, part-time staff members employed by the University, coordinate this effort. Mentors are supervised by a full-time, first-year experience coordinator. Building on student-to-student communication, a rapport is developed. Student mentors can provide empathy and break down possible barriers that may exist between staff members and students. At-risk students are then connected to the relevant support service that will assist them to get back on track (Figure 1). Student mentors will then follow up with the students with whom they have made contact, depending on their situation.

Regular communication both with student support staff and faculty is maintained via the computer database. In addition to this, regular meetings are held to provide faculty with updates of retention and completion issues.

The original intervention program began in our Health Faculty Department, in 2003, as a pilot project. Initial assessment of the results proved positive, and from 2004 onwards, the initiative was introduced into a number of other departments such as Hospitality, Social Sciences, and Education as a comprehensive intervention strategy. Likewise, initial interventions focused on students once they had commenced their studies. Further developments expanded these interventions to include contact with students before they began their studies at AUT (e.g., contacting students who had

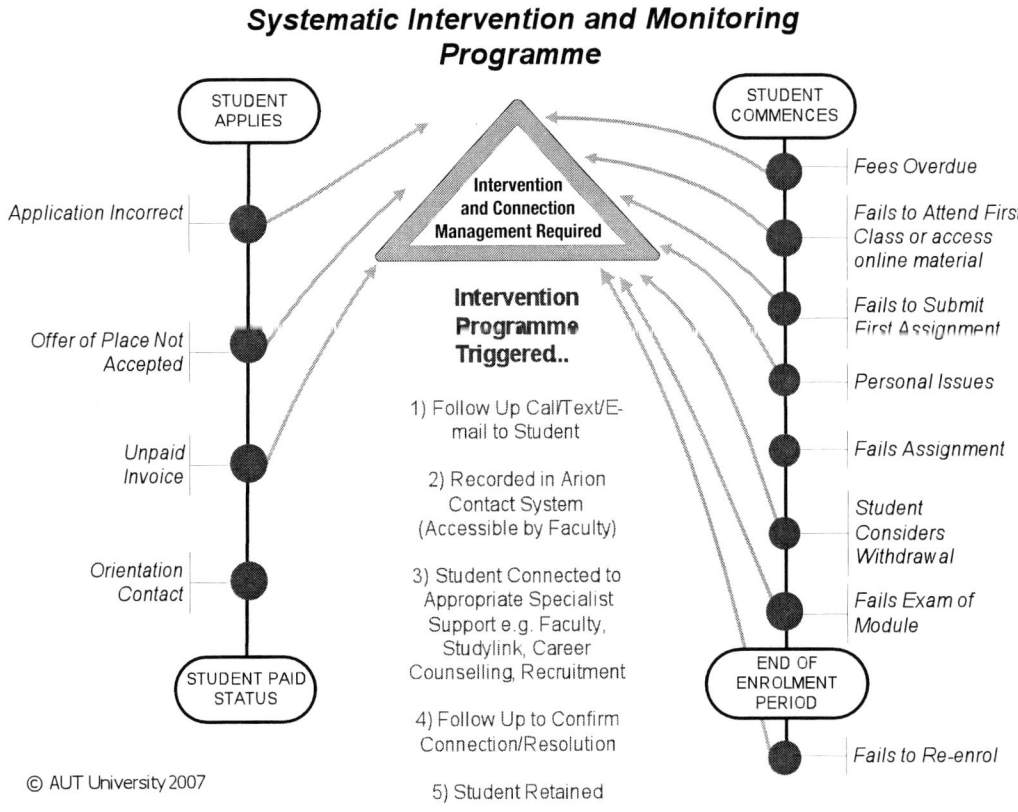

Figure 1. Intervention points and processes that connect at-risk students to specialist services. Copyright © 2007 Auckland University of Technology. All rights reserved.

unpaid fees, incomplete applications, or who had not accepted the offer to study at AUT). The major goals of this initiative were to provide holistic, proactive student support for at-risk first-year students. Through personalized contact, connections and access to relevant support services in the University would be enhanced for these at-risk students. This initiative would also assist with increasing retention and completion for **faculty**, subjects, and/or modules that report low retention and completion rates. Additionally, AUT would be able to provide meaningful data on retention and completion to student support services, and faculties.

Research Design

To evaluate the effectiveness of the initiative, a mixture of quantitative and qualitative data analysis was carried out. The original sample size consisted of 600 first-year undergraduate students studying in the Health Faculty. Additional schools became involved with the initiative after the original pilot project had been completed. Continuous evaluation of the initiative is carried out within each school and University-wide biannually.

At-risk criteria (i.e., incomplete or problematic applications, poor attendance, poor assessment **marks**) were defined before implementation. Several points during the student semester were noted as at-risk points, and personal intervention occurs at these times through e-mail and telephone communication. Students were flagged in the University's computer system, which then generated a report identifying those who were at risk. Any contact made with students was also recorded in this database.

Findings

The findings presented are relative to the context of New Zealand and Auckland University of Technology first-year students within the Faculty of Health. As such, they may not generalize to other institutions or settings. The use of a control group was not possible for this pilot study because of ethical concerns.

Quantitative Findings

Data collected from 2001 – 2004 demonstrate that retention and completion rates for students increased after the initiative was implemented in the Health Faculty. Figure 2 below demonstrates this increase in retention and completion rates for the Health Faculty from 2001-2004.

Figures 3-6 examine attrition, retention, and completion rates for students who received an intervention from the First Year Experience (FYE) Department and subsequently accessed additional support services. Figure 3 shows that students accessing the Learning Development Centre following an intervention had better completion and retention rates than those students who did not access additional learning support. Similarly, students who were referred to the Health and Counselling Centre (Figure 4) or the Career Centre (Figure 5) and who accessed those services performed better than students who did not follow up on the referral. Not surprisingly, students who accessed any student support service were more successful than students who accessed none (Figure 6).

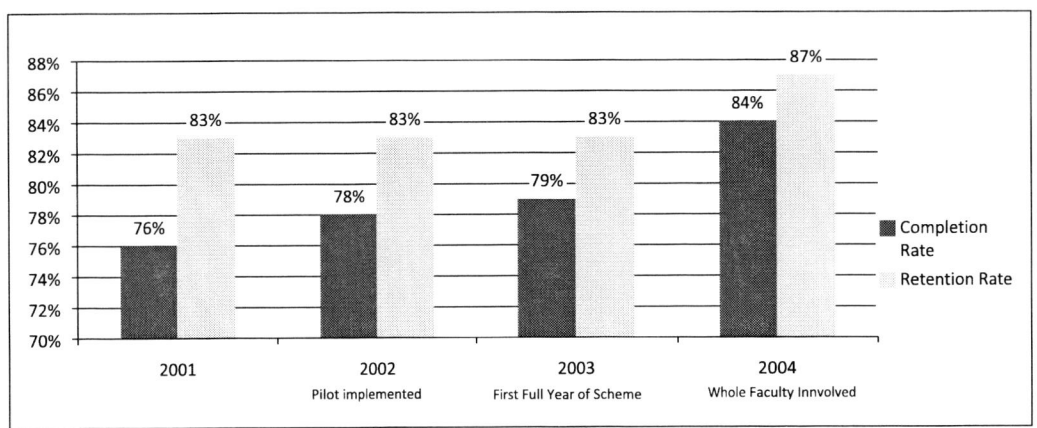

Figure 2. Health Faculty retention and completion rates for first-year students, 2001-2004.

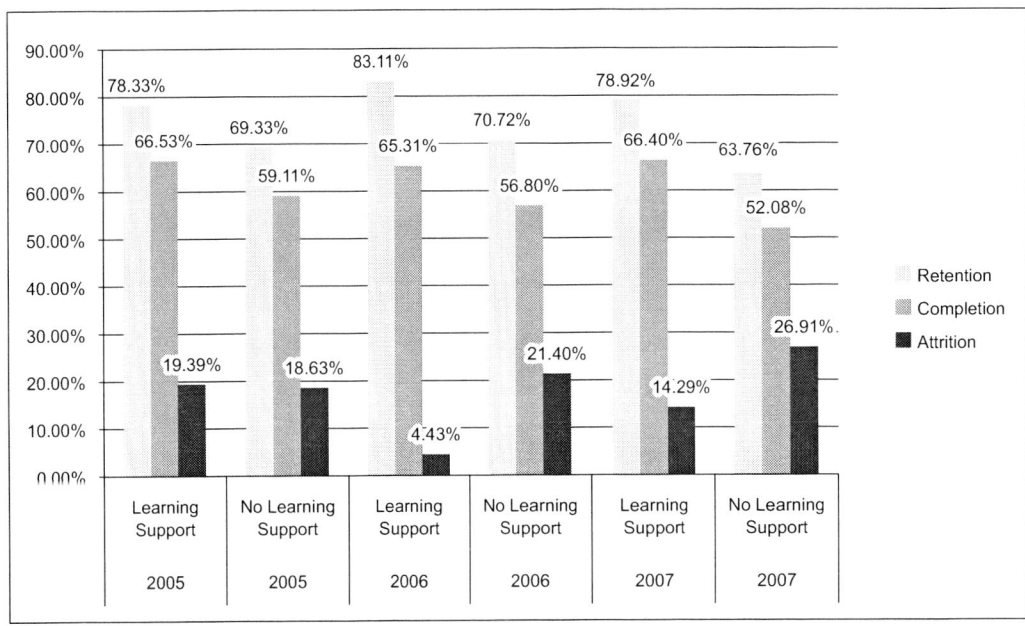

Figure 3. Retention, completion, and attrition rates for at-risk first-year students accessing learning support, 2005-2007.

Holistic Intervention Program 71

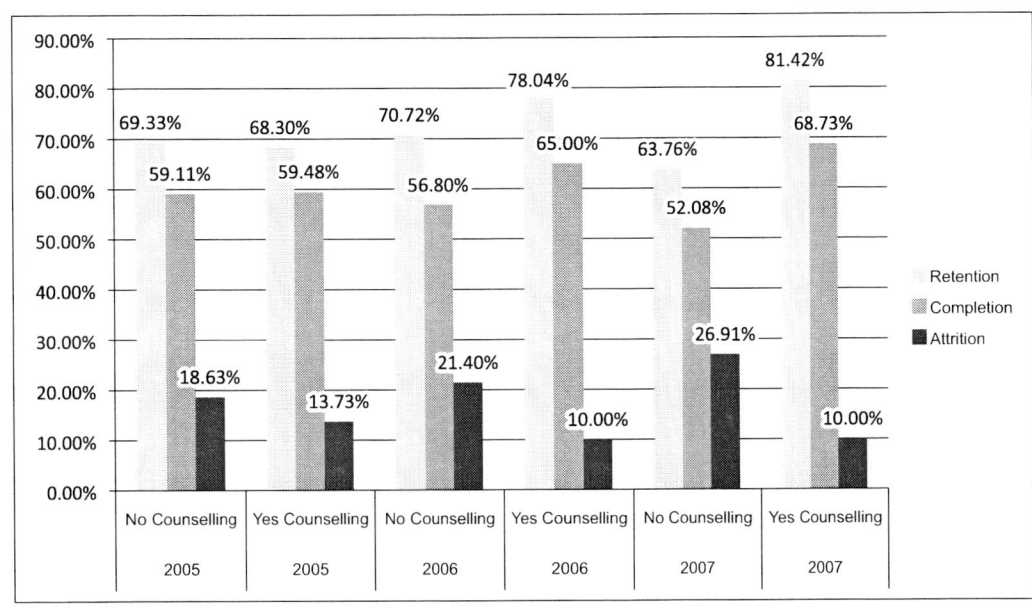

Figure 4. Retention, completion, and attrition rates for at-risk first-year students accessing counseling services, 2005-2007.

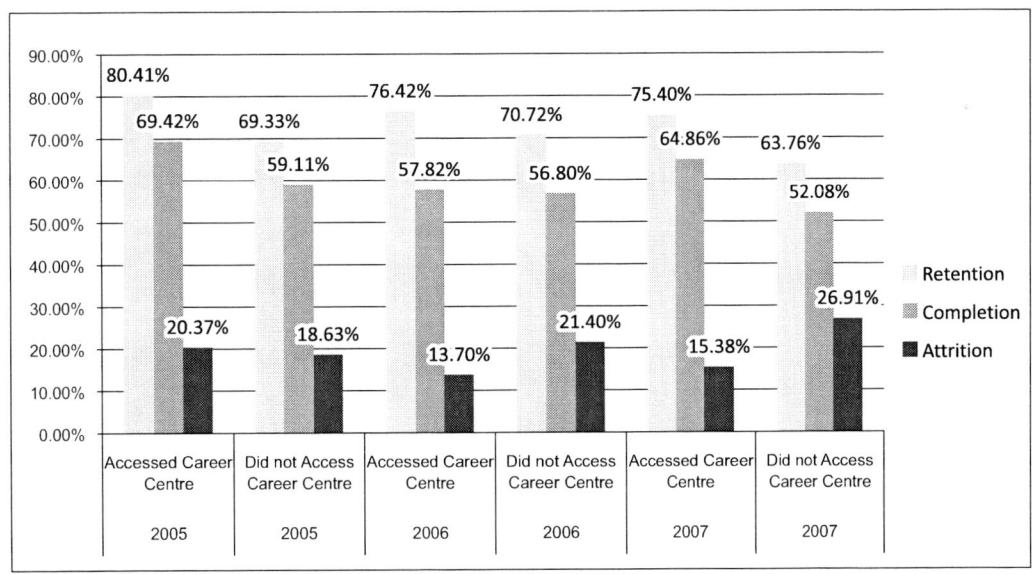

Figure 5. Retention, completion, and attrition rates for at-risk first-year students accessing career services, 2005-2007.

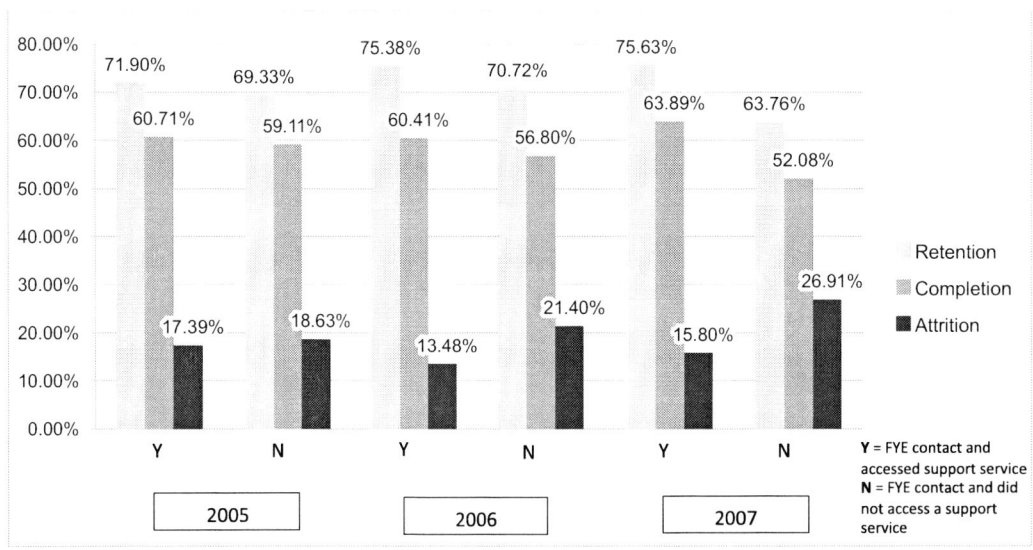

Figure 6. Retention, completion, and attrition rates for at-risk first-year students accessing any student support service, 2005-2007.

Qualitative Findings

Case studies were collected from 50 at-risk students who had prolonged contact with an FYE assistant during the pilot study. Three sample cases are provided below to demonstrate the impact this type of support has on students' experiences.

Student X. This student had a young family and was working nights. He was struggling financially; and as a consequence, he did not complete a compulsory class presentation. The student received repeated phone calls and was helped to connect with the **lecturer** who gave him an extension. The student completed and passed the paper. The lecturer commented on the usefulness of the intervention for the student:

> The student presented and was successful. He also offered his heartfelt appreciation for your follow-up that showed someone cared about him, and thus enabled him to pass his paper. He was very moved by such personalised support. So, credit to you and to those who enable the service you provide. It's neat to know that what you do makes a difference.

Student Y. After receiving personal information halfway through the semester that meant she would have to take a break from school, this student missed a compulsory test. After repeated phone calls, the student was referred to academic support where she was encouraged to finish the semester and apply for a leave of absence. The student also completed and passed her paper. Commenting on her experience with the initiative, the student noted, "On the whole, your help has really guided me through and has tremendously helped me put myself into proper perspective. I'd say that without you, I would have probably dropped out of the course…"

Student Z. Like many at-risk students, this student was contacted by FYE after failing to submit a compulsory piece of assessment. Following the contact, the student completed and passed the paper. Commenting on her experience with the intervention, the student noted:

> I had a really rough year last year and have been dealing with alcoholism and an eating disorder. Your service gave me a call and asked me whether my semester had gone well. I think the most important thing with your service was that you didn't just talk to me once—you called repeatedly, followed through, gave me all the information necessary, and I really felt supported and like you were on my side. The service was incredibly timely, and I am so grateful that you called me! I have a much greater understanding now of what is available at AUT.

This initiative demonstrates the impact that personalized, proactive contact can have on a student's experience and outcomes during their first year at university. The overwhelming response from students continues to be positive. A contributing factor to this has been students making contact with students. This approach enabled the development of a peer-based rapport and broke down any potential barriers to communication. In addition to this, the computer system that enables students to be tracked and their outcomes monitored has been an important aspect of the success of this initiative. This initiative used a phased approach to implementation, beginning with one school and then expanding after processes had been reviewed. This proved to be highly useful as any difficulties could be resolved at a lower level before moving to full implementation. Building faculty relationships during the initial phases was also crucial to the later success of this initiative. The further connection to specialist support services also proved to assist at-risk students with retention and completion. Those who accessed a support service were more likely to succeed.

Contributors

Gema Carlson
Manager, First Year Experience and Student Advisors
Auckland University of Technology
E-mail: gema.carlson@aut.ac.nz

Joanna Scarbrough
Director, Student Relations
AUT University
E-mail: joanna.scarbrough@aut.ac.nz

John Carlson
Director of Student Services
AUT University
E-mail: john.carlson@aut.ac.nz

NEW ZEALAND

Peer-Assisted Transition and Induction for First-Time Entering Undergraduates

The University of Auckland

The Institution and Its Students

The University of Auckland is the largest research-led university of New Zealand's eight public universities, enrolling approximately 38,000 students. It is both a residential and commuter campus in the heart of Auckland, New Zealand's largest city. The University's eight faculties offer 86 degrees at all levels. Undergraduates make up 24,200 of the total enrollment (82.6% of FTE students). Females outnumber males (58% vs. 42%), and 63.5 % of students are older than 24.[1] More than half (59%) of the students attend full time. The student body is ethnically diverse: 39% of students are of European ethnicity, 35% are of Asian origin,[2] 8% Pacific Islanders, 6.5% **Maori**, and 11.5% of students have not declared their ethnicity.

The Initiative

To improve the first-year experience and to increase the retention and progression rates of first-time entering undergraduates, the University of Auckland introduced an academic **induction** and campus socialization initiative in 2004. The UniGuide program embraces academic integration, social interaction, and personal aspects of campus life in groups led by senior students who serve as volunteer mentors, providing assistance and advice to new students during the first six weeks of the 14-week semester. The UniGuides inform and direct students to academic support, campus facilities, and services and encourage new students to participate in campus-wide activities. In this way, the UniGuides support and nurture new students during their transition to university life, personalizing the campus experience by putting a friendly, informed, and interactive interface in place for each new student in their UniGuide group.

In developing this program, the University adopted the Beatty-Guenter (1992) retention strategy model, adapting it and using it as a tool to inform and evaluate strategies and practices, identify strategy gaps, and evaluate transformational outcomes to facilitate successful, measurable, and progressive change. That is, we rely on the principles of sorting, supporting, and connecting groups of students in order to transform the student experience and the institution as a whole.

New students are invited to form small groups of 8 to12 people, sorted by **faculty**, and supported by a UniGuide. Assignment of students into groups is random, and groups can include clusters of self-selecting students from pre-existing personal, activity, or geographic relationships. This creates small, peer-mentored communities centered on the premise that for students to be fully integrated and involved in university life they need to develop a sense of belonging and an appropriate identity as a university student.

The initiative is designed to ease students' initial transition into the higher education sphere and to help them continue through higher education to the completion of their studies by improving their initial and ongoing socialization, adaptation to the campus ecosystem, and persistence with study.

Research Design

The retention and academic progress of those students who participated in the UniGuide program in semester one, 2004 ($n = 633$) was compared to a similarly sized control group of randomly selected students who enrolled at the same time ($n = 675$) but who did not participate in the UniGuide program. The study did not examine whether those who participate in the UniGuide program by choice are naturally more gregarious or are higher achievers who are more likely to persist anyway.

From these two groups, a longitudinal analysis of retention rates, persistence, and academic progress across an idealized three-year bachelor's degree curriculum was established. Retention was measured by comparing enrollment semester by semester. Academic progress was measured by the academic points completed in a semester. An annual load is the equivalent of 120 points, with Level One papers being 15 points, Level Two papers 20, and so on. A total of 360 points is required for a three-year qualification. A distinction was made between full- and part-time students: An annual enrollment of less than 100 points was considered part-time. Only students who participated in a bachelor's degree were included in the data analysis.

Findings

The value of a carefully crafted transition and retention strategy can be measured in many areas, none more important to a university than persistence and academic achievement. Longitudinal studies and ongoing research about the progress of initial UniGuide program participants showed that three years after implementation, the overall first-year dropout rate had fallen by almost 50%. Persistence rates continue to improve, and students are participating more in campus life. Improved retention and persistence outcomes of students who participated in the UniGuide program revealed that not only are higher percentages of the original cohort still enrolled and progressing, but these students are also completing qualifications at an accelerated rate compared to students who had not participated.

Retention

Six semesters (three years) and two summer schools after enrolling in February 2004, almost 85% of the UniGuide cohort remained enrolled, compared to 68% of the control group. This reflects a persistence rate 25% higher for UniGuide students. The retention differential (85% compared to 68%) over the idealized three-year degree program spectrum indicates that attrition for those in the UniGuide program was less than half (15% compared to 32%) of other students. The strategic value of this result is significant to both the University of Auckland and the education community at large (Figure 1).

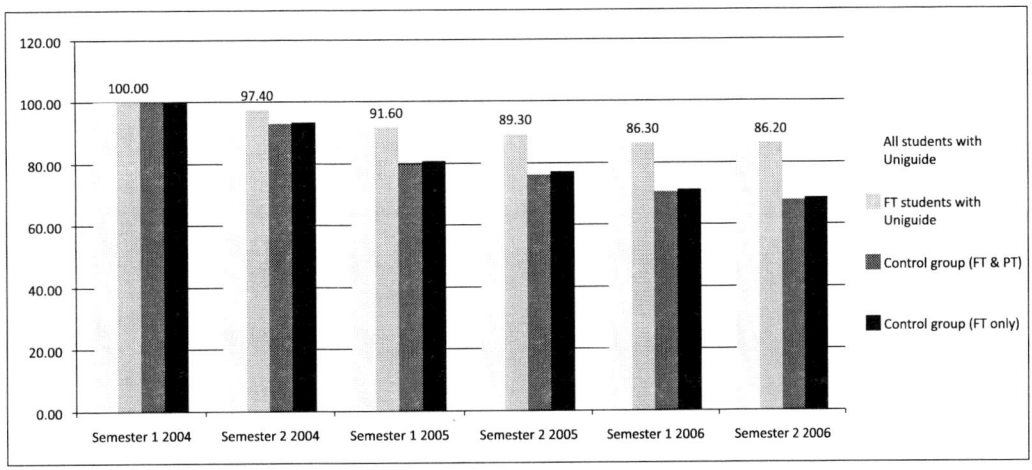

Figure 1. Percent of 2004 cohort retained, 2004 – 2006.

Academic Progress

The students who participated in the UniGuide program in Semester 1 2004 showed positive gains in academic progress compared to the control group. When analyzing the average points achieved by the end of the fifth semester, UniGuide students had achieved on average close to 30 points more than control group students. This may suggest that the type of student who volunteers for this program is more engaged, possesses more perseverance, and is more receptive to support. However, the results also clearly suggest that progress to completion and graduation was possible at an enhanced pace for proportionately more UniGuide students. By end of the sixth semester, UniGuide students had achieved on average 50 academic points more than the control group (Figure 2). Such fast-tracking capabilities—exemplified by UniGuide students—are a significant strategic advantage to both the students and the institution and are of particularly high financial relevance. That is, the risks of drop-out or failure are mitigated, and for both the student and the institution the return on investment is high.

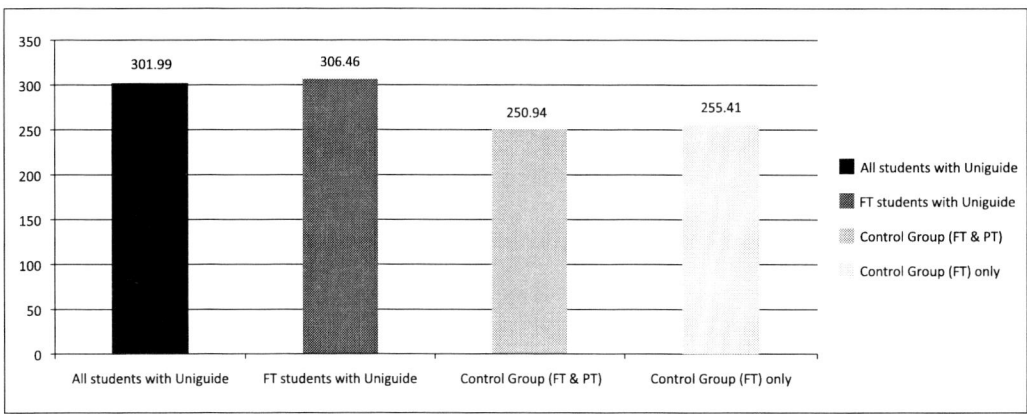

Figure 2. Mean cumulative academic points passed, 2004 – 2006.

Conclusion

The UniGuide program demonstrates that even where transition and induction are not embedded in the curriculum, transformation of both students and the institution can produce positive results. The return on investment is significant, not just in monetary terms, but also in terms of an enhanced first-year experience and overall student experience. Retention across the board has improved, and attrition is less than half the national trend for nonparticipants and significantly lower for UniGuide participants.

The program has achieved a number of important objectives that underpin and enhance the student experience and that also contribute to improved retention and persistence to graduation. For example,

- *UniGuides help students establish a sense of belonging (i.e., sorting factor).* A predisposition to be more social and more academically focused was not researched, and the study assumes that a skewing of data due to this is possible. For example, the control group is more likely to represent the full spectrum of age, gender, ethnic, and study status (e.g., adult, part-time, distance, online) than students in the UniGuide program, which is essentially for immediately postsecondary students. Nevertheless, with the intervention of a senior student as a mentor, students self-organize into communities with a general goal of supporting each other in the living and learning environment of the campus. Socialization, guidance, and control becomes distributed among participants. Specific roles of group members are not assigned but rather emerge from the interaction of the whole group who become a social learning community.
- *UniGuides help students form social networks (i.e., connectivity factor).* Research on learning communities (Cohen & Hoberman, 1983; McInnis & James, 1995; Tinto, 1975; 1987; 1996) suggests that, at least for traditional-age students, social integration may be a necessary precursor to academic integration. The collaborative nature of UniGuide communities, therefore, encourages students to become integrated both socially and academically.

- *UniGuides impact student retention (i.e., supporting factor).* Our studies of student retention indicate that students in UniGuide communities persist at greater rates than students who are not in these communities.
- *UniGuides improve academic performance (i.e., transforming factor).* The study has shown that students enrolled in UniGuide communities achieved improved performance compared to students who were not in communities: enrollment remained steady, persistence and progression occurred at an increased rate, and graduation occurred for a higher percentage of the UniGuide group than for the control by a significant margin. Approximately 67% of the UniGuide group graduated in three years, compared to 52% of the control group.

Implications

Strategically, the UniGuide program, measured in terms of retention, progression, and completion, has enhanced both the first-year experience and the overall student experience for the class of 2006 by providing greater interaction among students, their peers, and teachers and by allowing students to build the support relationships that they need to succeed.

From the University's perspective, the enhanced induction and monitoring of first-year students has increased retained revenue and added value to the University's brand, which has a national and international reputation for academic excellence. Significantly, the program delivered an improved student experience for an increasing number of its annual undergraduate population. Significantly, the importance of our transition and retention strategy, anchored as it is in the UniGuide program, has been fuelled by the changing financial nature of higher education. Since the mid-1980s, retention has been critical for institutions faced with shrinking budgets and increasing social pressure to provide a return on investment to the taxpayer public. Our estimate is that the program retains revenue of approximately NZ$2.5 million each semester. We have been running the program for nine semesters and estimate the cumulative value of retained revenue to be in tens of millions of (NZ) dollars.

Notes

[1] The University uses the categories: 18 or less, 19-20, 21-23, 24-29, 30-39, and 40+.
[2] This is a self-identifying ethnicity generally including mainland China, and the arc stretching from Japan, through Southeast Asia, the Malaysian Peninsula, up to and including the Indian Subcontinent.

References

Cohen, S., & Hoberman, H. (1983). Positive events and social supports of buffers of life change stress. *Journal of Applied Social Psychology, 13,* 99-125.

Beatty-Guenter, P. (1992). *Sorting, supporting, connecting, and transforming: Student retention strategies at community colleges.* Berkeley: University of California.

McMcInnis, C., & James, R. (1995). *First year on campus: Diversity in the initial experiences of Australian undergraduates.* Canberra: Australian Government Publishing Service.

Tinto, V. (1975). Dropout from higher education: A theoretical synthesis of recent research. *Review of Educational Research, 45,* 89-125.

Tinto, V. (1987). *Leaving college.* Chicago: University of Chicago Press.

Tinto, V. (1996). Learning communities and the reconstruction of the first year of college. *Planning for Higher Education, 25*(1), 1-7.

Contributor

Wayne Clark
Former Director of Student Administration
The University of Auckland
E-mail: Dr.Wayne.Clark@gmail.com

NORTHERN IRELAND

Enhancing Social Interaction Among Students and Staff Through the Use of Residential Events During Induction

University of Ulster

The Institution and Its Students

The University of Ulster is a publicly funded university in Northern Ireland, UK, with five campuses, each with its own mix of programs. The undergraduate population comprises about 17,000 FTEs, in a ratio of 4:1 full-time to part-time. These students are mainly local, and almost half of full-time students commute. The full-time undergraduate student body is 60% female, and 90% are traditional-aged students (under 21 years). The racial/ethnic makeup is predominantly White UK/Irish. Nearly half (47.4%) of traditional-aged students come from social classes NS-SEC 4-7 (i.e., National Statistics Socio-Economic Classification groups 4 to 7, small employers and self employed, lower supervisory and technical occupations, semi-routine occupations and routine occupations), reflecting the widening access mission of the University. About 40% of students are the first in the family to enter higher education, defined as having no parent, sibling, or close relation (aunt/uncle) who has previously enrolled in higher education.

The Initiative

The School of Environmental Sciences offers three honors degree programs in environmental science (30-35 students), geography (50-60 students), and marine science (10-15 students) and a two-year bachelor's degree that articulates with the other programs (10-15 students). Students in the two-year program can transfer to one of the honors degrees after successful completion of the **associate bachelor's degree**. More than 35 years ago, it was recognized that formal processes of **induction** needed to be supported by a significant social element but one that was also closely tied to **module** content and teaching. It was decided, therefore, to take all first-year students on a three-day, two-night residential field trip to the small town of Ardara in the south of Co. Donegal.

This takes place during the first week of teaching (teaching is suspended for that week). More formal induction events take place in the remaining two days on campus (see Table 1 for a schedule of activities). Each student pays £40 towards the cost of the accommodation; the School subsidizes the remaining costs. Including staff and transport, the total cost is about £65 per person. Because of the numbers involved and the limited accommodation, it is necessary to run the course twice (Monday to Wednesday and Wednesday to Friday) with different student groups.

Time in the field is spent doing field-based exercises in the countryside around Ardara in small groups with different **staff** leading parallel sessions. Thus, geography students evaluate the use of closed-circuit TV, examine the historical geography of a small settlement, consider the tourism development of Donegal Town (e.g., location and access, opportunities for recreation, accommodations and restaurants, tourist facilities), and look at river systems and do landscape interpretations. Environmental science students sample and evaluate plant biodiversity on cut-over bogs, examine the distribution of intertidal animals, and determine tree growth in forestry areas. Specific exercises change from year-to-year depending on the staff attending. Evenings are spent analyzing data and socializing (e.g., table quizzes). The work is supported by a handbook that provides background details for all the exercises, field methodology, and contribution to **assessment** later in modules (the assessment makes a 20% contribution to a module taken by all the cohorts). This handbook also contains all the learning outcomes and assessment criteria. Despite this emphasis on academic work and the assessment component, the field trip remains primarily an event where the students and staff socialize in an informal atmosphere. This helps to ease the students into fieldwork methods, particularly group work, where they begin to make friends and become comfortable with working cooperatively.

Research Design

The practice has been developed and refined over more than three decades and has been the subject of a number of formal and informal evaluations. It formed part of a study of fieldwork in seven institutions across the UK (Boyle et al., 2003) but has more recently been evaluated in its own right (McLaughlin, Southall, & Rushton, 2006). The focus of this latest evaluation (in 2005-2006) was to determine whether the practice was "fit for purpose," that is whether students benefited both socially and academically from the experience, and to determine if further refinement was necessary. A questionnaire was administered (adapted from Boyle et al.) both before the trip ($n = 52$, 40% response rate) and after the trip ($n = 71$, 54% response rate). These were followed up with a student focus group held during the term and interviews with key members of staff who are responsible for the organization of the event.

Findings

Although the field trip is an academic experience, its benefits in developing social contacts and breaking down feelings of isolation are of paramount importance and were the prime reason for instituting the practice originally. As Grosset (1991) indicates, students are more likely to commit to their course and institution if they feel part of a social group. Thus, one **lecturer** commented:

> I would put more emphasis on social bonding. Certainly, for the Donegal field trip the primary aim was to get the students to work as a group, to interact with members of staff and to get to

Table 1

A Typical Induction Week With a Residential Element Built Into the Start (Monday Through Wednesday Lunchtime)

	9:15 a.m.	10:15 a.m.	11:15 a.m.	12:15 a.m.	1:15 p.m.	2:15 p.m.	3:15 p.m.	4:15 p.m.	5:15 p.m. onwards
Monday	Welcome to the School	Travel by minibus to Donegal	→	→		Field exercise 1	→	→	Work up field data, social events
Tuesday	Field exercise 2	→	→	→		Field exercise 3	→	→	Work up field data, social events
Wednesday	Travel back to campus	→	→	Arrive back at campus	Skills audit	Sports and Freshers Fair	Sports and Freshers Fair	Sports and Freshers Fair	
Thursday	Introduction to Professional Development Planning	Introduction to WebCT	Careers	Plagiarism		Library and IT session (registration with computer system)	Photograph session		
Friday	Meet advisors of study, by appointment	The placement year	Meet advisors of study, by appointment						

know their colleagues more than anything else. If they became a happy working group in the first instance then that would continue through.

A staff member made a similar observation:

> We probably reduce the drop-out rate at an early stage, because a lot of students come and are concerned about leaving home. We do get homesickness. If people are left isolated, they are much more likely to be unhappy.

This is in contrast to the experiences of students in other programs, as another lecturer noted, "I think the big benefit is a social one. So many of them tell me that during practical classes they at least know another face. They talk to their friends in other courses, and they know nobody."

Quantitative analysis of the questionnaire responses supports this view (Table 2). Before the trip, the majority of students (84.7%) knew fewer than five other students. Afterwards, this had increased, and nearly 72% claimed to know more than 10 fellow students. They made friends through working in the field and through sharing accommodation. (Interestingly, room sharing was an initial anxiety with nearly one third of the students being apprehensive about this; this figure had dropped to only 8% afterwards.) The field trip also made a big difference to students' interaction with staff, with most students (87.3%) knowing between two and five members of staff afterwards compared with 75% who knew only one or no members of staff beforehand.

Table 2

Social Connections as a Result of Residential Field Trip

	% of students knowing other students				
Number of students known	None	1	2 - 5	6 - 10	> 10
Before (*n* = 52)	7.7	9.6	67.4	11.5	3.8
After (*n* = 71)	1.4	1.4	2.9	22.5	71.8
	% of students knowing staff				
Number of staff known	None	1	2 - 5	> 5	
Before (*n* = 52)	30.8	44.2	25.0	0	
After (*n* = 71)	2.8	1.4	87.3	8.5	

These findings were echoed in the student focus group meeting where one student said, "... I enjoyed it because I really got to know everybody, because I know lots of other girls [in other courses] who still know nobody in their class, whereas I'm confident that I know the majority in my class."

Despite the fact that one of the primary reasons for running the trip is to act as an icebreaker, the evaluation did highlight other benefits. It helped some students confirm their choices. For example, one student commented, "The field trip made me realize that this is what I want to do. It banished all the misgivings I had about not getting into Environmental Health. I really enjoyed it." It also helped some students realize quickly that they had made the wrong choice, and one or two have left as a result of this fieldwork experience.

Being thrown in at the deep end is not to everyone's liking, and some negative feedback was received. This largely related to logistics, geographical isolation, and quality of accommodation and food. Beforehand, there was a great deal of anxiety (i.e., 17% did not want to go and 44% were anxious about going), but afterwards this had largely evaporated (i.e., 80% were looking forward to more excursions). Overall, however, the staff and students believed that the trip fulfilled its aims.

Implications and Future Directions

This initiative has been in place for many years, and over time, it has evolved into the current model. The realization that there had to be a substantial and relevant academic component to the excursion was made some time ago, and now the assessment elements are firmly embedded in a common first-year module (Environmental Issues) taken by all students within the School of Environmental Sciences. Additionally, the field trip now also has its own learning outcomes and assessment criteria for the coursework. An important aspect is that the reports on the fieldwork that form the assessment are submitted by the end of Week 2, thus allowing the staff to monitor students' progress not only on the field course but also very early in their first semester. This contributes significantly to early identification of students who might be at risk of leaving the program before completion.

The exercises constantly change as different staff engage with the course, which adds to the diversity of its delivery. However, the general format remains unchanged. Due to limited accommodation, we have to present the course twice, and while students clearly integrate within their particular group, this does nothing to foster relationships between the two groups. Anyone thinking of adopting this format should try to ensure that all students are taken away together.

As a way of organizing part of induction, it is a transferable experience that could be applied to nearly all degree programs. For example, an interesting development, based on the Ulster model, has been that initiated by Norton, Larsen, and Walsh (2008) for health and applied science students at Liverpool Hope University in England. Here, more than 100 students spent a three-day, two-night stay at a residential outdoors pursuits center doing team-building activities such as rock-climbing. Unlike the Ulster model, there was no subject-related fieldwork, but reflective diaries completed by the students during and after the trip were summatively assessed in portfolio form and used during Personal Development Planning (PDP) sessions. Evaluation suggested this was also extremely effective in creating social bonding and a sense of belonging to the institution.

These shorter excursions (see also Pearce & McLaughlin, 2006) may be equally effective in promoting cohort identity. An interesting series of initiatives in psychology at the University of Sunderland in England (Westwood & Davies, 2008) testify to the importance of developing this aspect. As part of extended induction, a new student psychology society is proposing activities such as trips to sites of psychological interest (e.g., the Freud museum, old mental institutions) or film nights (e.g., screening of a psychologically- relevant mainstream film). They have also taken students to attend the British Psychology Student Members Group conference, and this was described as "a very positive experience" (Westwood & Davies, p. 91).

References

Boyle, A., Conchie, S., Maguire, S., Martin, A., Milsom, C., Nash, R., et al. (2003). Fieldwork is good? The student experience of field courses. *Planet, 5*, 48-51.

Grosset, J. (1991). Patterns of integration, commitment, and student characteristics and retention among younger and older students. *Research in Higher Education, 32,* 159-178.

McLaughlin, S., Southall, D., & Rushton, B. S. (2006). Residential events for induction. In A. Cook, K. A. Macintosh, & B. S. Rushton (Eds.), *Supporting students: Early induction* (pp. 27-39). Coleraine: University of Ulster.

Norton, B., Larsen, C., & Walsh, C. (2008). Residential field trip for health and applied social sciences students. In A. Cook & B. S. Rushton (Eds.), *Star projects: Embedding good practice* (pp. 61-83). Coleraine: University of Ulster.

Pearce, J., & McLaughlin, S. (2006). Off campus events for induction. In A. Cook, K. A. Macintosh, & B. S. Rushton (Eds.), *Supporting students: Early induction* (pp. 43-49). Coleraine: University of Ulster.

Westwood, D., & Davies, M. (2008). Extra-curricular opportunities for improving social interaction and commitment to the subject. In A. Cook & B. S. Rushton (Eds.), *Star projects: Embedding good practice* (pp. 61-83). Coleraine: University of Ulster.

Contributors

Brian S. Rushton
School of Environmental Sciences
University of Ulster
Coleraine
Co. Londonderry
BT52 1SA, Northern Ireland
Phone: 028 7032 4452
Fax: 028 7032 4911
E-mail: BS.Rushton@ulster.ac.uk

Suzanne McLaughlin
School of Environmental Sciences
University of Ulster

David Southall
School of Environmental Sciences
University of Ulster

Promoting First-Year Students' Learning Strategies Through Instructional Narratives

University of Minho

The University and Its Students

The University of Minho (UM) is a Portuguese public university. A total of 15,686 students attended UM in 2005-2006, including 1,249 enrolled in master's programs and 719 doctoral students (e.g., engineering, health sciences, law). Approximately 64% of the undergraduate students are local residents. About 70% of the traditional students have parents with no more than the minimum required schooling (9th grade). In the degree programs, there was an average dropout rate of 7.6%, defined as the number of continuing students who did not re-enroll in the academic year 2005-2006. Currently, as the University's primary focus is on increasing total enrollment rather than improving retention rates, efforts are being made to increase the number of students by attracting a more diverse applicant pool, especially students age 23 and older with some professional experience. UM allocates a 20% quota in degree programs for these students.

The Initiative

Approaches to learning refer to the relationship between students' motives and the strategies allocated to certain learning tasks (Rosário et al., 2005). Marton and Säljo (1976) presented two approaches to learning: surface and deep. Surface approaches include study behaviors guided by motives that are extrinsic to the learning task and strategies aimed at complying with the demands with the minimum time and effort. The deep approach develops from students' interest in the task and their commitment to maximizing meaning in order to expand understanding. These two approaches were identified and studied in different countries and across continents with several samples (Lonka, Olkinuora, & Makinen, 2004; Marton, Hounsell, & Entwistle, 1984). Although further research is needed to deepen our understanding of how students learn (e.g., the role of deep approaches in achievement), current academic challenges require us to promote high-quality outcomes at the university level in order to equip students with the appropriate tools to face labor world high demands. Aligned with the European universities, the University of Minho is facing the challenges of the **Bologna Process**, which stresses, among other aspects, students' autonomy and engagement in academic tasks. Lectures are assuming a less directive role, calling on students to increase their commitment with independent studying and agency. Demanding and proactive roles are expected to be assumed by students. This emerging academic culture appears as a huge challenge to the whole academic community, mainly to first-year students. The focus of our project is the promotion of students' agency as a means to deepen their commitment to learning and studying. The main challenge is how to enhance first-year students' self-regulation.

Course Description

The purpose of the present research was to investigate the effectiveness of a six-week learning-to-learn course by (a) analyzing the increase, if any, in students' declarative knowledge of learning strategies and (b) assessing the eventual changes, if any, in students' approaches to learning at the end of the course. One of the primary tools in the course is a textbook designed to help college students deepen their knowledge and practice of learning strategies. *Letters from Gervásio* (Rosário, Núnez, & González-Pienda, 2006), a Portuguese/Spanish research partnership outcome, is organized around the discussion of six letters, written by a first-year student to his belly-button, telling it about his experiences at the University (Rosário et al., 2007).

The letters are organized around clusters of self-regulated learning (SRL) strategies (e.g., setting goals, managing time, taking notes, dealing with test anxiety, learning memorization strategies). Table 1 outlines the letter topics and corresponding SRL strategies (Rosário et al., 2006). The narrative style lends this tool a dynamic character allowing for an ecologic adaptation to the specific learning context. The readers/authors have the opportunity to learn a broad range of learning strategies and to reflect about situations, ideas, and demands in context, as perceived by a student who lived through an academic experience similar to their own. This experiential closeness facilitates the discussion and acquisition of a perspective regarding the strategic contents introduced by the narrative. This shared, purposeful, and proactive self-reflection is intended to promote powerful adaptive qualities and may be the key to self-regulation.

As the final goal of this project is to help students to self-regulate and take control of their own learning, it works through the inherent rationale of the project, introducing a repertoire of SRL strategies spread throughout the letters (Zimmerman, 2002). Opportunities to rehearse and apply these strategies to different tasks and learning contexts are provided in each of the sessions.

Research Design

This project was conducted with 100 first-year college students from the Department of Economics who volunteered to participate in the project. Fifty-eight students enrolled in the course (experimental group), 35 female (60.3%) and 23 male (39.6%). Forty-two students, 29 male and 13 female (69% and 31%, respectively), served as a control group (not attending the course). In both groups, the mean age was 18 years. The experimental group was randomly chosen from the volunteers.

Table 1

Letter Topic and Corresponding Self-Regulated Learning Strategies

Letter Topic	SRL Strategy
Letter No. 1 *What does it mean, after all, adjusting to university life?*	Adapting to university Planning and time management

Letter No. 2
What are my goals? What really guides my actions at all levels, i.e., my studies, my university attendance, my hobbies, sport, and relationship with others... and even my laziness?
	Setting goals
	    Rules of goal setting
	    Short-term and long-term goals
	    Study goals and achievement goals

Letter No. 3
How can I take better notes?
	Organizing information (e.g., summaries, tables, diagrams, and conceptual maps)
	Note taking
	    The Cornell technique
	    Controlling distractions

Letter No. 4
Do you know how to fight procrastination, Gervase?
	Time management
	    To-do lists
	    Organizing the study environment
	    Procrastination
	    Relaxation techniques

Letter No. 5
Who rules your learning?
How can one tell successful students apart?
	Self-regulated learning
	    The cyclical model of SRL
	    Planning, execution, evaluation
	    Setting goals
	    Monitoring
	    Motivation

Letter No. 6
What is test anxiety?
How can one deal with test anxiety?
	Test anxiety
	    Aspects of anxiety (physical and emotional)
	    Internal and external distracters
	    Plagiarism and copyright
	    Relaxation techniques

This training program took place during the first semester of 2005-2006 in an **adjunct course format**. Training consisted of six, two-hour weekly sessions that met after the scheduled class. In small groups of 20 to facilitate the discussion, students read a letter and were asked to discuss and work on the SRL topics presented in the narrative. In order to organize the information, the instructor ended the sessions by summarizing the main topics.

Instruments

The Approaches to Learning Inventory (*Inventário de Processos de Estudo - IPE*, Rosário et al., 2005) is a 12-item instrument designed to assess college students' deep and surface approaches to learning, organized on a five-point Likert scale ranging from 1 (*not at all true for me*) to 5 (*very true for me*). For example, surface motivation is captured by items such as "The best way to get good grades is to repeat the ideas presented by teachers in class." Deep strategies are captured by items such as "I study every day over the semester and review my notes regularly." Alpha for the deep approach scale is 0.72 and 0.70 for the surface approach scale.

The Declarative Knowledge of Learning Strategies Questionnaire (*Questionário de Conhecimento Declarativo de Estratégias de Aprendizagem - QCDEA*) (Rosário et al., 2006) is a 10-item multiple-choice questionnaire that addresses the most important learning strategies practiced in the course (e.g., cognitive and metacognitive strategies, anxiety, and time management). The final score in this variable (i.e., learning strategy declarative knowledge) corresponds to the sum of questions answered correctly.

Procedure

Students in both groups completed the IPE and the QCDEA twice (i.e., at the beginning and end of the course sessions). This paper focuses on the analysis of these pre- and posttest data in order to reach some conclusions about the efficacy of the course in promoting learning and studying strategies.

Findings

The first and main purpose of this research was to assess the efficacy of the intervention. Paired *t*-tests were conducted, which revealed statistically significant increases in students' learning strategies knowledge in the experimental group ($t_{55} = -3.432, p = .001$), but not in the control group ($t_{41} = -.286; p = .777$).

The second goal of the research was to acknowledge the students' approach to learning before and after completing the course. Data show that students in the experimental group obtained lower scores on surface approaches to learning at the end of the course ($M_{dif} = 10.24$), these differences being statistically significant ($t_{55} = 13.362, p = .000$). Students in the control group did not show statistically significant differences ($t_{41} = -.075; p = .940$). Table 2 provides the means and standard deviations for both declarative knowledge and approaches to learning.

Regarding deep approaches, the residual mean differences in the experimental group did not reach statistical significance ($t_{55} = 1.117, p = .269$); this also was true for the control group ($t_{41} = 1.03; p = .306$) (Table 2).

Aimed at increasing students' metacognitive reflection, this course is anchored on a narrative framework (e.g., the discourse of a first-year student [like them] about his academic experiences, the discussion of useful learning strategies, and problem solving). Students' activities after reading and discussing the letters are designed to enhance the practice and application of learning strategies

Table 2

Pre- and Posttest Means and Standard Deviations for Declarative Knowledge and Approaches to Learning ($N = 100$)

	Experimental group ($n = 58$)				Control group ($n = 42$)			
	Pretest		Posttest		Pretest		Posttest	
	M	*SD*	*M*	*SD*	*M*	*SD*	*M*	*SD*
Learning strategy declarative knowledge	8.04	1.52	8.71	1.32	7.52	1.45	7.55	1.54
Surface approaches to learning	23.36	3.14	13.02	3.30	16.60	4.00	16.70	4.85
Deep approaches to learning	21.81	3.49	21.38	3.49	20.20	3.12	19.80	4.16

and to improve self-regulation processes (e.g., time management by reflecting on the amount of time spent, wasted, and saved in a week; goal setting by allocating daily tasks and activities to personal academic and social goals; note taking by analyzing the main ideas and topics listed in a lecture by different students).

In this six-session course, both reflection and practice proved to have promoted not only the enrolled students' declarative knowledge of learning strategies and self-regulation processes but also to have decreased their reliance on surface approaches to learning as compared to the control group. However, findings did not reveal adoption of deeper approaches to learning. This could be due either to the short duration of the intervention (only six sessions) or to the responsive nature of the approaches to learning as they act as mediators of situational interpretations (e.g., instructional, personal, and contextual variables, such as frequency and nature of the **assessments**, academic expectancies, and personal goals, among others, influence students' approaches to learning and the quality of the outcomes).

Implications

Although using different design and assessment instruments, these findings corroborate results from previous studies (Hofer & Yu, 2003; Núñez, Solano, González-Pienda, & Rosário, 2006; Rosário et al., 2007), which stress the importance of managing strategies that are designed to promote learning how to learn. Further research is needed to track students' self-regulated learning processes (e.g., diaries and metacognitive reflections; see Schmitz & Wiese, 2006) but also to develop new educational tools and to design interventions that promote students' self-regulation and maximize learning (Rosário et al., 2006).

This program, as with similar ones focusing on learning processes, can be successfully used in the welcoming initiatives designed to facilitate first-year students' academic integration and well-being.

References

Hofer, B., & Yu, S. (2003). Teaching self-regulated learning through a "learning to learn" course. *Teaching of Psychology, 30*, 30-33.

Lonka, K., Olkinuora, E., & Makinen, J. (2004). Aspects and prospects of measuring studying and learning in higher education. *Educational Psychology Review, 16*, 301-323.

Marton, F., Hounsell, D. J., & Entwistle, N. J. (1984). *The experience of learning*. Edinburgh: Scottish Academic Press.

Marton, F., & Säljo, R. (1976). On qualitative differences in learning: Outcomes and processes. *British Journal of Educational Psychology, 46*, 4-11.

Núñez, J. C., Solano, P., González-Pienda, J. A., & Rosário, P. (2006). Self-regulation processes measurement through self-report methodology. *Psicothema, 18*(3), 353-358.

Rosário, P., Mourão, R., Núñez, J. C., González-Pienda, J. A., Solano, P., & Valle, A. (2007). Eficacia de un programa instruccional para la mejora de procesos y estrategias de aprendizaje en la enseñanza superior. [Evaluating the efficacy of a program to enhance college students' self-regulation learning processes and learning strategies]. *Psicothema, 19*(3), 353-358.

Rosário, P., Núnez, J., & González-Pienda, J. (2006). *Comprometer-se com o estudar na Universidade: "Cartas do Gervásio ao seu umbigo"* [Committing to study at university: Letters from Gervase to his belly-button]. Almedina.

Rosário, P., Núnez, J., González-Pienda, J., Almeida, L., Soares, S., & Rúbio, M. (2005). El aprendizaje escolar examinado desde la perspectiva del "Modelo 3P" de J. Biggs. [Academic learning view from the perspective of John Biggs' "3P model"]. *Psicothema, 1*(17), 20-30.

Schmitz, B., & Wiese, B. (2006). New perspectives of training sessions in self-regulated learning: Time series analyses of diary data. *Contemporary Educational Psychology, 31*, 64-96.

Zimmerman, B. J. (2002). Becoming a self-regulated learner: An overview. *Theory Into Practice, 41*(2), 64-70.

Contributors:

Pedro Rosário (primary contact)
Assistant Professor
Departamento de Psicologia da Universidade do Minho, Campus de Gualtar, 4710
Braga – Portugal
Phone +351 962418871
E-mail: prosario@iep.uminho.pt

Rosa Mourão
PhD Student
Departamento de Psicologia da Universidade do Minho, Campus de Gualtar, 4710
Braga – Portugal
E-mail: miamourao56@hotmail.com

José Carlos Núñez
Professor
Departamento de Psicología de la Universidad de Oviedo
Plaza Feijoo s/n
33003 Oviedo
Phone: + 351 985103217
E-mail: jcarlosn@telecable.es

Júlio González-Pienda
Professor
Departamento de Psicología de la Universidad de Oviedo
Plaza Feijoo s/n
33003 Oviedo
Phone: +351 985103217
E-mail: julioag@uniovi.es

António Valle
Professor
Facultade de Ciencias da Educación
Campus de Elviña, A Coruña
Phone: +351 981167000
E-mail: vallar@udc.es

SOUTH AFRICA

The First-Year Academy: An Institution-Wide Initiative to Foster Student Success

Stellenbosch University

The Institution and Its Students

Stellenbosch University (SU) is a medium-sized, research-led public institution offering a range of three- and four-year degree programs as well as a six-year medical program. Situated in the university town of Stellenbosch in the Western Cape, South Africa, SU has approximately 24,000 students, with 14,800 undergraduate students and just over 4,000 first-years. The undergraduate population is predominantly white (77%) and comprises 52% female students. The age profile is particularly homogenous with only 4% of students being over the age of 25. Approximately 30% of the first-year cohort is made up of first-generation students. The University is renown for its student life with more than one third of the undergraduate population living in student residences and another one third of students living in private accommodations in town. The balance of the students commute.

In recent years, high first-year attrition rates as well as increasing numbers of students taking longer than the minimum time to complete their degrees have been cause for concern at the University. Although there had always been pockets of activity across the University that sought to improve student retention and academic achievement, these interventions were often ad hoc and piecemeal, and thus had limited impact on the University as a whole. It became clear that if any significant change was to take place, a more systemic approach that incorporated the entire University community was needed. In response, at the start of 2006, the University embarked on an extensive process to review its first-year experience, which led to the establishment of the First-Year Academy.

The Initiative

The First-Year Academy (FYA) is an overarching framework that has as its main objective the promotion of first-year success. It provides a focus on the coordination of university-wide activities and supports **faculty-specific** interventions that have this same aim. Such a systemic-holistic approach is based on the premise that student success is not exclusively determined by what happens in the lecture rooms but also by what happens outside the lecture rooms (see Astin 1985; 1996; 1997; McCuskey & Dunkel, 2006). In practical terms, this means that every aspect of the students' experience of university life impacts their chances of achieving success and is the reason why the entire University, including residence life, sport, community engagement, and recreation has been made part of the scope of the FYA. From its inception, the FYA enjoyed the full support of the University's top management, and one of its key goals has been to engender ownership and ensure participation among all stakeholders across the campus.

It was a huge challenge to get the whole University to participate and be involved in such an initiative, but two structural interventions contributed significantly toward ensuring involvement and ownership over a wide spectrum: (a) the creation of Teaching and Learning Coordination Points (TLCs) in all faculties, where academic and support staff meet regularly to discuss matters affecting the success of first-year students, and (b) the establishment of a First-Year Academy Committee as a subcommittee of the Teaching and Learning Senate Committee. Within these newly formed structures, a number of specific interventions to facilitate first-year success were implemented. Significant among these were the development of a prediction model for first-year success and the Early Assessment System, which requires that all first-year students complete an **assessment** task or tasks in each of their modules during the first six weeks of the academic year. The results from these largely diagnostic and formative assessment activities are collated within less than a week so as to provide a holistic picture of the student's academic standing, for both the student and the **lecturer**. In this way, students receive an early warning as to potential areas of concern, while lecturers and tutors can respond more directly to students' needs and offer more focused support.

Research Design

In the short time that the FYA has been in existence, the various initiatives that fall within its scope have been subjected to ongoing review, monitoring, and evaluation as part of a four-year study that will be completed in 2010. This case study reports on initial findings in this long-term intervention. The aim of the longitudinal study is two-fold: to determine (a) whether there has been effective coordination of activities and interventions within the FYA and (b) whether these have enhanced the retention and success rates of first-year students. The evidence being shared here has been drawn from a number of sources. Faculty reports, the minutes of faculty TLCs and the quarterly FYA Committee meetings, and focus groups, provide qualitative data. Quantitative data has been drawn from the student tracking system, which presents a 10-year picture of first-year student results, including data on 2006 and 2007—the conceptualization and implementation years of the FYA. It is important to emphasize that at this early stage we highlight trends and describe initial perceptions and understandings that have emerged from the first phase of the evaluative process. We are acutely aware of the complexity that comes with seeking to evaluate a project of this magnitude.

Findings

To bring about the sort of institutional change that would be required to implement the FYA, it is crucial that there is an understanding among the different stakeholders of the nature of the change and implications it carries, for the change to be feasible, and for ongoing feedback on the change process to be provided (Nadler, 1987; Kirkpatrick, 1998; Kotter, 1996). Throughout 2006 and 2007, therefore, much time and effort was channeled into addressing this need. Twenty different TLC meetings, five Committee meetings, and six focus groups were held to discuss, debate, and review different initiatives within the FYA. The minutes of these meetings provided evidence of a growing understanding as time progressed. A key indicator of this change in attitude emerged in the discourse around the FYA, particularly with regards to the Early Assessment System, which was described as "a positive barometer," "a strategic tool," "a process of identification," making "students more aware," and "very valuable."

A change in practice was also evident in the increase in the number of requests by lecturers for funding to undertake research into their own teaching and assessment.[1] This has led to a number of individual initiatives linked to specific modules and/or specific academic departments—all seeking to enhance student success.

The data on student retention and success rates would appear to suggest that the focus on the first year, the shifting of perceptions among academics, the ongoing support from University management, and the many activities that are being implemented under the FYA umbrella are bearing fruit. Figure 1 details the percentage of credits passed for all first-year students over the past 10 years. This graph clearly shows the decrease in achievement during the 2003-2005 period that led to the introspection and eventually the establishment of the FYA in 2006. The results of 2006 and 2007 (the first full year of implementation), on the other hand, show a reversal of the earlier downward trend.

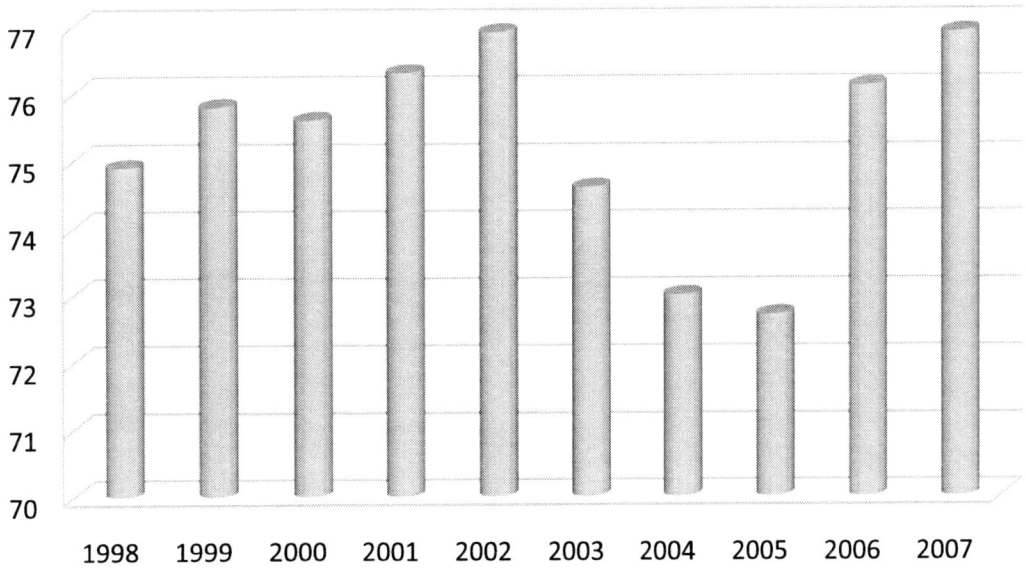

Figure 1. Percentage of credits passed by first-year students, 1989-2007.

Similarly, Figure 2 shows the poorer retention rates for the 2003-2005 period, but registers a significant increase for 2006 (87.6% over 84.5% in 2005). Although the 2007 figures indicate a drop of 2% from the 2006 highpoint, it is still the second highest rate recorded for the 10-year period. In addition, it should be noted, that in 2007 two large faculties increased their readmission requirements thus making it more difficult for students who were performing poorly to return.

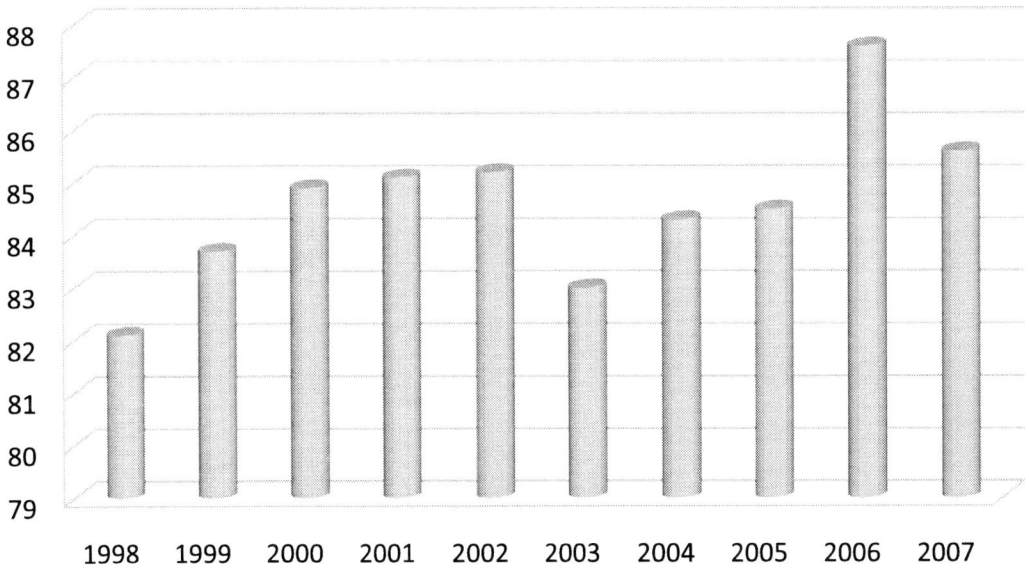

Figure 2. Retention rates, 1989-2007.

Having a clear benchmark for success and retention rates over a significant period of time is of particular value for the FYA. However, it remains incumbent on those responsible for the evaluation process to carefully contextualize these data and acknowledge the many different variables that impact student success.

Implications

The implementation of the First-Year Academy has significant implications for Stellenbosch University, many of which continue to manifest as challenges that will need to be addressed as the initiative continues to grow. It will be important to sustain momentum across the University and to ensure the necessary resources and support for the many tutor and mentor programs, research projects, learning community programs, Early Assessment System, and the many other activities that fall under the FYA umbrella. Recent changes in the national school curriculum and national school-leaving certificate will add to the complexity of the ongoing evaluation of this work.

Nevertheless, much has been learned during the past few years, lessons that could be of value to the broader FYE community. It is important to have the support of the institution's management (an important factor in our achievements thus far at Stellenbosch), to have faculty-wide buy-in, and to have the resources to support the different initiatives. Instituting structures that create faculty-based platforms from which to launch the work of the FYA has also been crucial and has played a key role in engaging faculty. Finally, it would appear that providing students with early warning of their academic standing and responding to this early warning with appropriate support, which has been possible through our early assessment strategy, can lead to improved student success.

In establishing a systemic, university-wide initiative to support the first-year experience, Stellenbosch University has created a unique synergy that paves the way for potentially powerful collaborations across the campus in the interest of student success.

Notes

[1]FIRTL (Fund for Innovation and Research into Teaching and Learning) is an internal, SU fund made available to lecturers to support the Scholarship of Teaching and Learning.

References

Astin, A. W. (1985). *Achieving educational excellence*. San Francisco: Jossey-Bass.

Astin, A. W. (1996). Involvement in learning revisited: Lessons we have learned. *Journal of College Student Development, 37*(2), 123-134.

Astin, A. W. (1997). How "good" is your institution's retention rate? *Research in Higher Education, 38*(6), 647-658.

Kirkpatrick, D. L. (1998). *Evaluating training programs: The four levels* (2nd ed). Berrett-Koehler Publishers: San Francisco.

Kotter, J. P. (1996). *Leading change*. Boston: Harvard Business School Press.

McCuskey, B. M., & Dunkel, N. W. (2006). *Foundations: Strategies for the future of collegiate housing*. Columbus, Ohio: The Association of College & University Housing Officers International.

Nadler, D. A. (1987). The effective management of organization change. In J. W. Lorsch (Ed.), *Handbook of organizational behavior* (pp. 358-369). Englewood Cliff: Prentice Hall.

Contributors

Ludolph Botha
Senior Director
Academic Support
Stellenbosch University
Private Bag X1
Matieland, 7601
South Africa
Phone: +27 +21 8083751
E-mail: hlb@sun.ac.za

Susan van Schalkwyk
Deputy Director
Centre for Teaching and Learning
E-mail: scvs@sun.ac.za

SWEDEN

The SciTech Model: From First Year to Career

Uppsala University

The Institution and Its Students

Uppsala University is a research-intensive, public university that accepts students from all parts of Sweden. In 2006, 4,200 FTE undergraduate students were enrolled at the Faculty of Science and Technology. Of these, 36% were women, and 36% were at least 25 years old. In Sweden, ethnic and academic background information is not collected at the institutional level. However, our first-year student survey indicated that 70% of the new science and technology students had at least one parent with a university education.

The Initiative

The SciTech (science and technology) model aims to counteract dropout and improve student progress towards a degree and is based on a number of key concepts. These concepts include personal contact, access to information, and an understanding of academic life. Personal contact between new students and **staff** is crucial, and a personal touch has also been given to all information material including our web site. During their first term, students often experience information overload so we always strive to provide accurate information when needed. Our students come from all over Sweden, and for many of them, this is their first time away from home. Therefore, we highly prioritize an introduction to academic life. In addition, we regularly monitor our students' progress and level of satisfaction with their studies in order to discover and counteract problems at an early stage.

Figure 1 shows a schematic depiction of the SciTech model. The activities start before enrollment and continue throughout the educational programs, either three years for a bachelor's degree or five years for a master's degree. A detailed description of the activities is provided below. Regular monitoring of student results enables the prompt introduction of extra support for individual students as required and provides useful quality **assessment**. The model is complemented by a number of learning activities along the way.

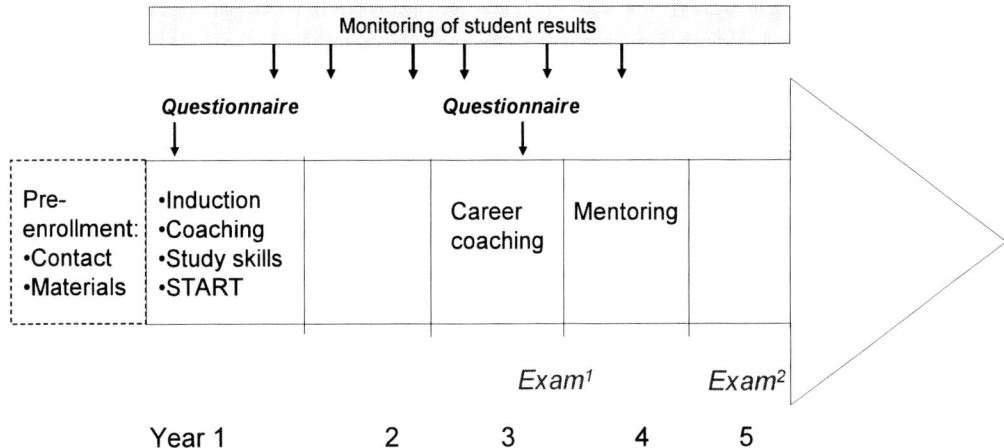

Figure 1. The SciTech model extends from pre-enrollment until the third-year[1] bachelor's degree or the fifth-year[2] master's degree.

Pre-enrollment Activities

To ensure that newly accepted students receive accurate information, we send a welcome letter one month before enrollment. New students also receive a phone call from an older student the week before enrollment to welcome them.

First-Year Activities

To welcome new students, a one-week, voluntary **induction** organized by the student union follows enrollment. Induction activities include guided tours of Uppsala and the student clubs, social activities, and refresher courses. In the week after induction, students fill out a questionnaire providing us with information about their previous education, parents' education, and reasons for choosing their study program. We also ask them to evaluate our information materials and recruitment activities.

Academic counselors coach new students as well as support and introduce them to academic life. During the early stages, coaches have group meetings with their students where the coach describes the study program; highlights differences between lectures, seminars, and laboratory work; reviews rules and regulations; and discusses practical issues such as student health care and **accommodations**.

This period is followed by a course in study skills integrated into a core science, math, or technology course that the coach teaches in cooperation with regular **lecturers** in order to maintain contact with students. The course deals with reading, writing, and problem-solving skills as well as how the brain and memory function, motivation theory, study habits, and planning.

The START peer support program, which is designed to facilitate social and academic integration, encourages contact between new and more advanced students. In this program, a group of new students meets with a second-year student (START leader) for study sessions or to talk about academic issues during the autumn term. START leaders participate in leadership and group dynamics training and receive regular support by University staff.

Activities During Subsequent Years

The **faculty** has recently developed career planning support services with counselors as career coaches. Third-year students are offered a series of seminars in which they practice writing curriculum vitae, learn to network, and reflect on their personal skills and preferences. In the third year, students are also asked to answer a web-based questionnaire to assess their overall satisfaction with their studies.

A pilot mentoring program for fourth-year students is presently under development. The aim of this program is to increase student contact with prospective careers. To emphasize the transition between studies and profession, we recruit young, recently graduated engineers and scientists to act as mentors.

Monitoring Student Progress

As an important part of the model, academic counselors regularly monitor individual student progress by assessing the number of earned credits. First-year students receive progress reports and are contacted and offered individual guidance if necessary. The monitoring of second- and third-year students is based on the number of academic credits earned in August/September. Students are contacted and offered individual guidance and a follow-up meeting is scheduled in February if needed.

Research Design

New activities are developed as pilot projects and carefully evaluated before full implementation. Once implemented, these projects are subject to regular assessment.

We evaluated all pilot projects using qualitative and quantitative methods that included surveying students' impressions of the initiatives and analyzing dropout rates and student progress. All students in all initiatives filled out questionnaires. To allow students to elaborate on and explain their opinions, we interviewed a group of student representatives or allowed them to participate in focus groups with questions exploring how the initiative was perceived and whether the initiative was useful to them.

As a quantitative measurement, we calculated the percentage of newly registered students who earned more than 37 credits in their first year of study, which is the minimum requirement for receiving the Swedish national student loan to cover living expenses (the nominal figure for a full-time student in Sweden is 60 credits per year). It was used here as a marker for successful studies because failing to receive the student loan makes studying considerably more demanding, since students are then forced to support themselves by other means.

Findings

All the projects described below began as pilot programs and are now regular activities. Coaching was introduced as a pilot project in 2004-2005. Approximately one third of the students participated in coaching, which was voluntary. Of the 118 students responding to a questionnaire, approximately 48% felt the coaching program was useful or very useful to them (Figure 2). Participating students appreciated coaching, as evidenced by comments such as, "It's good because it shows you care about us."

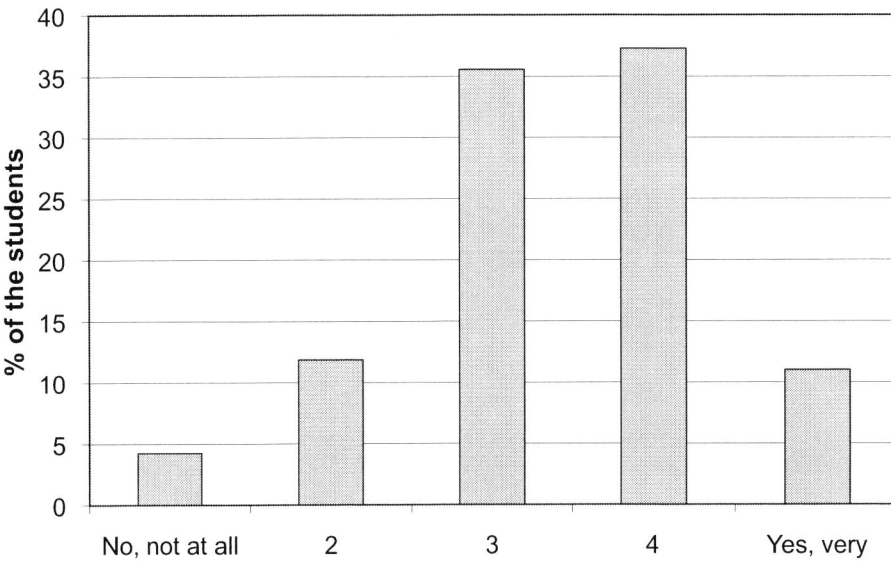

Figure 2. Percentage of students agreeing that coaching program was coaching useful, 2004-2005 ($N = 118$).

The course in study skills, also introduced in 2004, received an even better response. Asked their general opinion of the course, 59% of the 259 students responding to the questionnaire in 2006-2007, when it was introduced on a regular basis, rated it "good" or "very good" (Figure 3). To date, some 850 students have taken part in the course, and the best results were achieved when the coach-lecturer partnership was well-coordinated and cooperation functioned smoothly.

START was introduced in 2005 and was the initiative most appreciated by the students. As one student commented, "That's the great thing about START—you learn how to study from someone who was recently in the same position as you are now." Of the 104 students responding to the questionnaire, 80% of them agreed or strongly agreed that the program had fulfilled its objectives (Figure 4).

Career support is very popular with students, and the response to the career coaching pilot project offered in 2007 was very positive. In the spring of 2008, the project was available to all technology students in revised form.

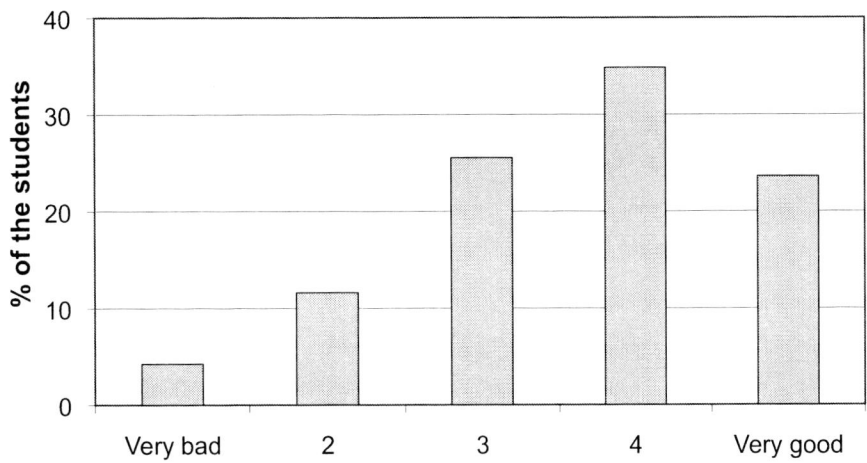

Figure 3. Student assessment of the study skills course, 2006-2007 ($N = 259$).

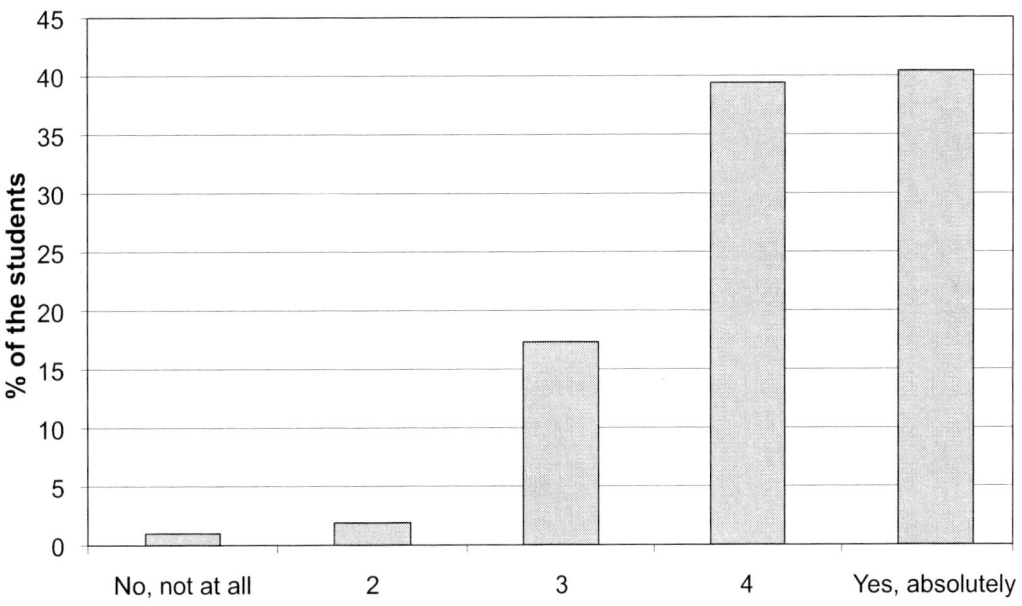

Figure 4. Percentage of students agreeing that START objectives were met, 2005-2006 ($N = 104$).

Since introducing coaching, the study skills course, the peer support program START, and the regular monitoring of student results by academic counselors, the proportion of students earning more than 37 credits has increased slightly (Figure 5). Because these are measures to be taken in the long-term, this ratio may well increase further.

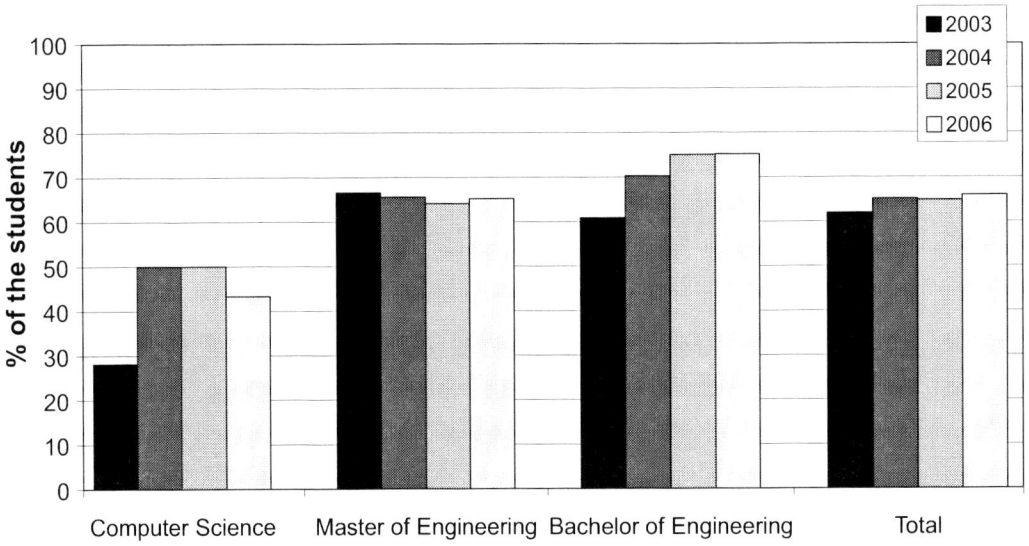

Figure 5. Percentage of students earning at least 37 credits during the first year of study, 2003-2006 ($N = 2{,}721$).

Implications and Future Directions

Based on our experience of the SciTech model and participating student evaluations, we can draw some conclusions for how this initiative should be formed to obtain successful results. First, it is important to establish good contact with students from the beginning and to create a friendly atmosphere. Successful coaching is highly dependent on personal chemistry and timing. Success comes when coaches/study counselors manage to have constructive, positive contact with students. The outcome of the study skills course is also dependent on an open dialogue among the coach, lecturer, and student. It is an additional advantage if the lecturer is interested in pedagogical innovation.

Regarding the START peer support program, it is important to strike a balance between social and academic activities in order to support students effectively and to motivate them to continue to meet. START also helps identify students with academic difficulties and/or other problems at an early stage. It is extremely important to assess student success, progress, and academic satisfaction early on. A system for an even earlier follow-up than in our model would be of great interest.

The implementation of this initiative has taught us that it is very important to involve lecturers in pedagogical development while developing other retention activities, and to have a pedagogic approach in all stages of planning. In summary, it is crucial that the work described in the SciTech model coincides with classroom initiatives and pedagogical development.

Elements of, or the entire, SciTech model could be adapted by other institutions with only minor local adjustments. The initiative in its entirety is better suited for longer study programs, but parts, such as coaching or the study skills course, could easily be applied as one-time efforts.

Based on information obtained in coaching sessions and from various surveys, we know that students find it difficult to connect their studies with a future professional career. Work is in progress to make the professional perspective an integral part of the programs. For instance, we have initiated specific projects designed to address these issues, such as the mentoring project mentioned in which students and industry mentors meet regularly. Our long-term goal is to make all students comfortable with their university education and to create opportunities for academic success. Our goal also includes lowering the dropout rate and having 80% of first-year students achieve 37 credits or more during their first year, with maintained course quality. We will continue to support students of the Faculty of Science and Technology with the SciTech model with special emphasis on first-year students. We are now also extending our model to include new projects focused on activities related to future professional life and careers.

Contributors

Maria Orvehed
Director
Uppsala University, Faculty of Science and Technology
External Relations Section
Box 550
SE-751 22 Uppsala, Sweden
Phone: +46 18 471 6808
Fax: +46 18 471 6864
E-mail: maria.orvehed@uadm.uu.se

Eva Söderman
Senior Faculty Administrator
Uppsala University, Faculty of Science and Technology
Office of Administration, Uppsala School of Engineering
Box 536
SE-751 21 Uppsala, Sweden
Phone: +46 18 471 6398
Fax: + 46 18 471 3000
E-mail: eva.soderman@uadm.uu.se

UNITED STATES OF AMERICA

Assessing Student Learning in Freshman Inquiry

Portland State University

The Institution and Its Students

Portland State University is situated at the south end of downtown Portland, the largest city and metropolitan region in the state of Oregon, USA. The University is a four-year, public, commuter campus that is developing a residential population as well. In fall 2007, the undergraduate full-time equivalent was 18,938 students. In fall 2008, there was a 9% increase in first-time, first-year students for a class of 4,485 (40% new to college and 60% transfers). As is customary for PSU, almost half the entering class was first-generation college attending, meaning that neither parent had graduated from college. The ethnic composition of the institution is shown in Table 1. The institutional gender percentages are 46.5% men and 53.5% women, numbers that align with national college enrollment statistics. The average age of first-time students in fall 2008 was 18.9. The average age of the entire undergraduate student population at PSU is 25.3.

The Initiative

The distribution model of general education is the basis for liberal education in most universities in the United States. It consists of a menu of **courses** that students choose from to meet a required number of credits taken in each of the liberal arts areas (i.e., the sciences, humanities, and social sciences). The assumption is that students will leave the University with a grounded understanding of the world and her/his place in it as well as the deep disciplinary knowledge of her/his major. The reality is that students choose courses based on openings in their schedules and have little understanding of why they are asked to take those courses. A faculty task force charged with examining Portland State's general education curriculum in the early 1990s found no philosophical basis for the distribution model or any research supporting it.

Table 1

Ethnic Breakdown of Portland State University Undergraduate Population, 2008-2009 (N = 18,983)

Ethnic Origin	Number	Percent
American Indian	252	1.3
Asian/Pacific Islander	1,815	9.6
Black, Non-Hispanic	620	3.3
European American	12,167	64.2
Foreign Students*	114	0.6
Hispanic/Latino	891	4.7
International Students	927	4.9
Multiple Ethnicities	362	1.9
Declined to Respond/Unknown	1,790	9.5

*Students enrolled at PSU's overseas campuses.

As a result, PSU implemented a new program for general education called, University Studies (UNST) (http://www.unst.pdx.edu) in fall 1994. The four-level, inquiry and goal-based program took advantage of the emerging research on student learning and on general education, integrating what they found into the design of the program. For example, in Astin's (1993) research, some of the key factors he found to have a positive effect on student learning were interactions among students and between students and faculty, a student-oriented faculty, student tutoring programs, and opportunities to discuss racial/ethnic issues with other students. The program attempts to maximize its impact on student learning by limiting class size to 36 students and encouraging high faculty/student interaction through active-learning pedagogies. Peer-led sessions of no more than 13 students supplement course meetings and provide opportunities for students to tutor and guide one another.

Community-based learning, active and project-based pedagogy, and technology-enriched classrooms were melded into a multidisciplinary curriculum focusing on four goals of general education: (a) inquiry and critical thinking, (b) communication (written, oral, visual, quantitative, group, technological), (c) the diversity of human experience, and (d) ethical issues and social responsibility. The last two goals connect directly to Astin's (1993) factor of involving students in discussions on racial and ethic issues. Under the goal of the diversity of human experience, students are expected to "enhance their appreciation for and understanding of the rich complexity of the human experience through the study of differences in ethnic and cultural perspectives, class, race, gender, sexual orientation, and ability." The programmatic definition of Social Issues and Ethical Responsibility is that "students will expand their understanding of the impact and value of individuals and their choices on society, both intellectually and socially, through group projects and collaboration in learning communities."

The course, which is required for the majority of entering students and which serves as the basis of PSU's first-year experience program, is Freshman Inquiry (FRINQ). It is a three-term course with the curriculum created around themes designed by interdisciplinary groups of faculty, each paired with an undergraduate student peer mentor. Examples of current themes are Design and Society, The Columbia River Basin, The Work of Art, Ways of Knowing, and Sustainability. In each theme, readings, class discussion, assignments, and projects connect the specific theme to the four goals of general education. The students meet twice weekly in a large group with the course faculty and her/his mentor. In addition, each student mentor hosts two sessions a week for 13 students who meet in rooms with a central conference table surrounded by individual computer terminals. Each member of a FRINQ team is also expected to deliver at least one session each term to the other classes within the theme. In this way, students get to know one faculty member very well, as they stay in the course together for the entire first year. Exposure to others on the instructional team increases opportunities for faculty/student interaction and, possibly, the student's connection to the institution.

Research Design

Because University Studies was such a new type of program and such a departure from the distribution model, it was important to assess the work at the program level to ascertain whether it was accomplishing its goals. A variety of methods have been used to assess the effectiveness of FRINQ, and the **assessment** plan or its instruments have changed based on earlier findings or because of specific requests from faculty. The current assessment plan, which has been in place since 1999, has now been integrated into the regular work of the program with the director, Freshman Inquiry faculty coordinator, and the research analyst supporting and carrying out the activities. When appropriate, faculty, student mentors, and staff across the institution are invited to participate in the assessment efforts. The activities related to program effectiveness are the end-of-year student survey and the e-portfolio review. Together, the results of these show evidence of actual classroom practices and student-reported learning outcomes in the four goal areas. The e-portfolio review compares student work from the classrooms against program-wide rubrics to determine whether the entering student class is performing at an acceptable level at the end of the year.

The FRINQ program assessment includes three primary methods, described in greater detail below. Table 2 illustrates the timing of the various assessments and their primary function. For example, formative assessment efforts are designed to demonstrate to the teaching faculty what is working or not in the class with time in the term to make changes that will affect the final learning outcomes. Summative assessment activities are used for program and faculty evaluation.

1. *Prior Learning Assessment (formative).* The Prior Learning Assessment (PLA) is an online survey that asks about students' academic experiences prior to attending PSU, reasons for and concerns about attending college, and early college experiences and plans. The survey results provide information to individual faculty members about their students and to the program about the overall preparation and needs of the incoming first-year class. Questions are added by specific themes that will then be revisited on the end-of-year class surveys. In this way, the PLA serves as a pre/postassessment for learning in thematic areas. During the first two weeks of fall 2007, 1,276 Freshman Inquiry students (86% response rate) completed a PLA.
2. *FRINQ End-of-Year Survey (summative).* The FRINQ End-of-Year Survey is an online survey administered during the mentor sessions, which asked students to rate their experiences in their FRINQ course over the 2007-2008 academic year. Students responded to questions about the course format, faculty pedagogical practices, and mentor contribution to the

course. We look at those factors found in the Astin's (1993) research that contribute to enhanced student learning and satisfaction. The results provide information to individual faculty about their course and to the program about students' overall experience in FRINQ. These questions also speak to an institutional concern about retention. During the final three weeks of spring term 2008, 741 FRINQ students (64% response rate) completed the End-of-Year survey.

3. *FRINQ Portfolio Review (summative).* Throughout the FRINQ courses, students develop portfolios representing their work and reflecting the relationship of that work to the four general education goals. Faculty have developed a standard, end-of-year e-portfolio assignment that all the thematic teams use. Students choose work they have done over the year that demonstrates their learning in each goal. They write a reflective essay describing why they chose particular work samples for each goal. Students also reframe each goal in her/his own words. This practice helps students internalize and make meaningful the goals of general education. The final piece is a reflective essay discussing the student's learning over the entire year. The FRINQ Portfolio Review process scores student portfolios against rubrics developed to measure student learning related to those goals. The results provide information to faculty teams about student learning in FRINQ themes and to the program and University on students' overall learning in FRINQ. During spring 2008, students were asked for permission to evaluate their portfolios as part of program assessment for University Studies. Of the 1,157 students enrolled in FRINQ in the spring, 678 (58.5%) returned consent forms, and 469 (69.2%) of those returning forms gave consent. Of these, 210 student portfolios were randomly selected for review representing 30 portfolios for each of the seven FRINQ themes. When electronic portfolios with bad URLs were excluded, 196 portfolios were reviewed. In 2008, the portfolio review process focused on the Critical Thinking goal and the Ethics and Social Responsibility goal. Each goal was assessed using a six-point rubric, where six is a score expected of a graduating senior (http://www.pdx.edu/unst/goals.html). The expectation is that FRINQ students will score at a 2 or 3 by the end of their first year. In addition to using the rubrics, each portfolio was assessed against a checklist developed to provide information about the types of assignments included in student portfolios. Inter-rater reliability for the Ethics and Social Responsibility rubric was 86% and 81% for the Critical Thinking rubric.

Table 2

Freshman Inquiry Program Assessment Plan

Academic Level	Fall	Winter	Spring
Freshman Inquiry (FRINQ)	Formative: Prior learning assessment (all FRINQ sections)	Formative: Early term assessment (optional)	Formative: Early term assessment (optional)
	Early term assessment (required for new instructors, optional for returning instructors)	Summative: Mid-year assessment	Summative: End-of-year assessment
	Summative: End-of-year assessment		E-portfolio review

Findings

In general, students agreed that they had opportunities to address all four of the University Studies goals in their FRINQ courses. Means on these items ranged from 3.74 to 4.11 on a five-point agreement scale. When looking at the percentage of students who agreed or strongly agreed with those items, over two thirds of students responded in their way. For all items, mean scores increased from the 2006-2007 school year to the 2007-2008 school year (Table 3).

Students also generally agreed with statements about their faculty members' teaching practices. These practices demonstrate high faculty/student interaction and active-learning strategies. All items had means above 3.0 on a five-point scale. Students were most likely to agree that faculty expressed a personal interest in their learning ($M = 4.01$) and used a variety of methods to evaluate student progress ($M = 3.98$). Students were less likely to agree that faculty inspired them to set and achieve challenging goals ($M = 3.51$), explained course material clearly and concisely ($M = 3.51$), or made it clear how each topic fit into the course ($M = 3.55$). Table 4 provides student responses on these items for 2006-2007 and 2007-2008.

Over the last three reviews, the mean Ethics and Social Responsibility score was consistently between 2 and 3 on a six-point scale. Mean Ethics scores across the seven FRINQ teams ranged from 2.27 to 2.75. Over the last three reviews, the mean Critical Thinking score was consistently around 3 on a six-point scale. Mean Critical Thinking scores across the seven themes ranged from 2.42 to 3.14 (Table 5).

Table 6 provides information on the kinds of documents students included in their portfolios and the relationship of that information to the critical thinking and social responsibility goals. Almost all students (95%) included evidence of personal narrative, and a large majority included analytical writing and used appropriate grammar in their portfolios (87.9% and 83.5%, respectively). About half of students included research papers and graphs and charts in their portfolios (59.2% and 48.1%, respectively). The number of students including evidence of assignment instructions (19.2% vs. 41.6%) or a first draft (8.4% vs. 34.4%) increased dramatically from 2006-2007 to 2007-2008.

When reviewing data related to Ethics and Social responsibility, we found that most students included ethical scenarios (64.2%), identified specific social issues (75.7%), and made connections between issues and personal choices (55.9%). A critical essay was the most frequently included piece of evidence in the Ethics and Social Responsibility section of the portfolio (61.9%), while PowerPoint presentations and statistical analyses were included by far fewer students (8.1% and 15.4%, respectively).

Related to Critical Thinking, most students included statements of their own positions (88.3%) and outside evidence to support their positions (61.1%). Fewer students provided evidence of identifying multiple positions (43.4%) and evaluating those positions in a coherent argument (22.4%). The most frequently included types of evidence of Critical Thinking were the critical essay (58.2%) and informal response papers (59.9%). Again, PowerPoint presentations and statistical analyses were the least frequently included type of evidence for Critical Thinking (13.1% and 27.4%, respectively).

Table 3

Student Perceptions of Learning Outcomes in FRINQ

In the FRINQ course students had the opportunity to…	2006-2007 ($N = 667$)		2007-2008 ($N = 741$)	
	Mean	Std. Deviation	Mean	Std. Deviation
Apply course material to improve critical thinking	3.95	0.87	4.05	0.89
Acquire skills in working with others as a member of a team	4.01	0.87	4.07	0.87
Explore issues of diversity such as race, class, gender, sexual orientation, ethnicity	4.11	0.90	4.13	0.91
Develop skills in expressing myself orally	3.74	0.95	3.86	0.94
Develop skills in expressing myself in writing	3.98	0.89	4.08	0.91
Learn how to find and use resources for answering or solving problems	3.81	0.91	3.93	0.89
Learn to analyze and critically evaluate ideas, arguments, and multiple points of view	3.97	0.88	4.08	0.91
Explore ethical issues	4.04	0.89	4.09	0.98

Note. Ratings made on a scale of 1 = Strongly disagree to 5 = Strongly agree.

Table 4

Student Perceptions of FRINQ Faculty

The FRINQ Faculty...	2006-2007 (*N* = 667)		2007-2008 (*N* = 741)	
	Mean	Std. Deviation	Mean	Std. Deviation
Displayed a personal interest in students and their learning	4.01	0.99	4.09	0.98
Scheduled course work (i.e., class activities, tests, projects) in ways which encouraged students to stay up to date in their work	3.63	1.12	3.83	1.01
Formed teams or discussion groups to facilitate learning	3.91	0.97	4.05	0.90
Made it clear how each topic fit into the course	3.55	1.14	3.69	1.12
Explained course material clearly and concisely	3.51	1.18	3.65	1.13
Related course material to real life situations	3.78	1.04	3.90	1.03
Inspired students to set and achieve goals which really challenged them	3.50	1.07	3.69	1.09
Asked students to share ideas and experiences with others whose backgrounds and viewpoints differ from their own	3.90	1.00	4.01	0.99
Provided timely and frequent feedback on test, reports, or projects to help students improve	3.71	1.06	3.86	1.05
Encouraged student/faculty interaction outside of class (e.g., office visits, phone calls, e-mail)	3.82	0.98	3.91	1.01
Used a variety of methods (e.g., papers, presentations, class projects, exams) to evaluate student progress	3.98	0.94	4.09	0.93

Note. Ratings made on a scale of 1 = Strongly disagree to 5 = Strongly agree.

Table 5

Mean Portfolio Scores on Selected University Studies Goals

	Academic Year					
	2002-2003 (N = 150)		2005-2006 (N = 198)		2007-2008 (N = 196)	
	Mean	SD	Mean	SD	Mean	SD
University Studies Goal						
Critical thinking	3.10	.70	3.00	0.9	2.89	0.82
Ethics and social responsibility	2.53	.85	2.80	1.0	2.44	0.87

Table 6

Analysis of Portfolio Content

	2006-2007		2007-2008	
	N	Percent	N	Percent
General Portfolio Evidence				
Personal narrative	177	87.2	180	95.2
Analytical writing	179	88.2	167	87.9
Creative writing	62	30.5	66	33.7
Research paper	*		116	59.2
Graphs and/or charts	*		89	48.1
Assignment instructions	39	19.2	79	41.6
Evidence of a first draft	17	8.4	65	34.4
Appropriate use of grammar throughout	153	75.4	157	83.5
Evidence Related to Ethics and Social Responsibility				
Ethical scenarios	*		120	64.2
Connection between issue and personal choices	*		105	55.9
Identification of specific social issue	*		137	75.7
Research paper	*		67	35.8
PowerPoint	*		15	8.1
Critical essay	*		117	61.9
Statistical analysis	*		29	15.4

Continued on p. 117

Table 6 continued

	2006-2007		2007-2008	
	N	Percent	*N*	Percent
Evidence Related to Critical Thinking				
States own position	*		166	88.3
Identifies and examines multiple positions	*		79	43.4
Provides outside evidence in support of positions	*		113	61.1
Evaluates multiple positions in a coherent argument	*		41	22.4
Research paper	*		80	42.3
PowerPoint	*		25	13.1
Critical essay	*		110	58.2
Statistical analysis	*		52	27.4
Informal writing or response paper	*		112	59.9

*Not collected in 2006-2007

Implications

Since the beginning of our assessment efforts, the findings have suggested that students are achieving the learning goals associated with University Studies and that our current efforts are more effective than those in the past. As part of the assessment plan, the data and analysis from each activity is reviewed by the director and by the FRINQ faculty leadership. The assessment report also goes to the FRINQ faculty in their teams who then revise their curriculum in response to the findings. If the results show deficiencies across the program, new initiatives to strengthen a particular goal area become part of the following year's activities. For example, in response to lower than desirable qualitative literacy scores, faculty members responded by identifying quantitative literacy assignments and classroom strategies used by faculty who scored highly in that area. The assignments and classroom strategies of high-performing faculty members are shared with others so that they can be adapted for other themes. When the e-portfolio reviewers found a lack of evidence on the writing process, the common end-of-year e-portfolio assignment was revised to include samples of the students' writing process, not just the final products.

Many other universities have now adopted portions of the design of University Studies and even its complete design. Many have also chosen to adopt the way the program is assessed, the mentor program structure and training, and faculty development activities for their own institutions. The FRINQ courses transfer to other institutions. The recommended credit breakdown is found on student transcripts.

References

Astin, A. W. (1993). *What matters in college: Four critical years revisited.* San Francisco: Jossey-Bass.

Contributors

Judith P. Patton
Associate Dean, School of Fine and Performing Arts; Professor, Theater Arts/Dance
Director, University Studies, 2000-2006
Portland State University
P.O. Box 751
Portland, Oregon 97207-0751
Phone: 503-725-8367
E-mail: pattonj@pdx.edu

Rowanna Carpenter
Research Analyst, Office of Research and Institutional Planning and University Studies

UNITED STATES OF AMERICA

The Efficacy of a Coordinated, Multilayered First-Year Experience Program

Purdue University

The Institution and Its Students

With more than 72,000 students across its four-campus system, Purdue University is one of the 20 largest institutions of higher education in the United States. The University's main campus, which occupies more than 2,300 acres and 160 major buildings in West Lafayette, Indiana, had an enrollment of 40,090 students during fall 2008. This included 31,761 undergraduate and 8,329 graduate/professional degree students. This case addresses first-year experience-related efforts occurring on Purdue University's West Lafayette campus, and for that reason some additional context on that campus is merited.

The University is truly an international institution with a reach spanning across the globe. During fall 2008, the West Lafayette campus' student body included more than 5,479 international students from over 125 different countries, giving Purdue one of the top three international student enrollments among public institutions in the United States. In addition to a large international student body, the University reflects the racial diversity of the state of which it is a part. For example, in fall 2008, Purdue's undergraduate student body included 3,936 students who identified themselves as being African American, Asian American, Hispanic, or Native American—12.4% of the overall undergraduate population. Approximately 42% of all undergraduate students are female. The majority (70.7%) of the domestic student body are Indiana natives, while 29% come from a state other than Indiana. The new class of first-year students varies between 6,500 to 7,500 students a year based on enrollment management goals with roughly one quarter of these students being from the first generation of their respective families to attend college. This large and diverse student population resides in one of the 16 different on-campus residential options operated by the University or in an array of nearby apartments or houses. The majority (more than 90%) of first-year students live on campus.

With historical strengths in engineering and agriculture—the University was founded in 1869 as Indiana's land-grant college—Purdue's West Lafayette campus presently offers more than 7,400 courses in a given year in over 500 undergraduate majors and specializations. These majors and specializations yield degrees in the Schools or Colleges of Agriculture; Consumer and Family Sciences; Education; Engineering; Liberal Arts; Management; Pharmacy, Nursing, and Health Sciences; Science; Technology; and Veterinary Medicine. Many of these programs are regarded among the best in the United States and the world, as evidenced by *U.S. News, London Times, Princeton Review,* and other forms of rankings that routinely place many of Purdue programs among the top 10 of their kind.

The Initiative

As the size of the institution might suggest, Purdue University is very complex. Historically, the University has functioned as a collection of highly autonomous colleges, and thus it was not uncommon for students who majored in one college or academic program to have a first-year experience that was radically different from students who majored in another. However, in the 1990s, amidst growing national interest in enhancing the first-year experience, Purdue University began to take a series of steps to coordinate its array of first-year initiatives, recognizing that this coordination would create positive synergies for students, create a core of common experiences across the University, and eliminate unnecessary duplication. A major catalyst for the effort came in fall 1997 when the University was awarded a $5 million grant from Lilly Endowment, Inc. to fund 10 different retention initiatives. This five-year funded effort resulted in the establishment of a robust University-wide learning communities program, the foundation of a series of interdisciplinary honors courses that became the basis of the University's Honors Program, the expansion and enhanced coordination of **orientation** programming for undergraduate first-year and transfer students, the creation of a Supplemental Instruction program, the launch of an array of discipline-specific first-year seminars, as well as the formation of an office to coordinate many of these University-wide efforts. Upon completion of the grant, after taking into account the data from a series of rigorous **assessments** that showed students who participated in the programs had significantly higher retention rates, the University continued to support the aforementioned efforts with recurring institutional funds.

In fall 2005, further efforts were undertaken to enhance coordination of learning and support initiatives for first-year students when several distinct entities, including the coordination office associated with the former Lilly Endowment-sponsored retention initiatives, were amalgamated into one new department—Student Access, Transition, and Success Programs (SATS). The mission of the SATS department is to empower and inspire all students to embrace a sense of life-long learning by providing student-centered, precollege preparation and college success initiatives and services. These initiatives assist students in their preparation for, transition into, and success in the Purdue environment—with a heavy emphasis on the first-year experience. The department's various interconnected and mutually reinforcing programs assist students in progressive stages of development and have as their ultimate goals an increased rate of student degree completion, future employment or study, dedicated citizenship, and responsible leadership in the state, nation, and world. Some of the major efforts housed in the SATS department, and the focus of this case, include:

◇ Boiler Gold Rush, the University's week-long orientation program that occurs before the start of the first semester. Most recently, 5,355 new first-year students (75% of the first-year class) participated in Boiler Gold Rush.

- Summer, Transition, Advising and Registration orientation programs, a series of one-day advisement and registration programs for new students attended by approximately 92% of all domestic first-year students and transfers during summer 2009
- University's coordinated learning communities, an academic program in which first-year students co-enroll in two or more of the same course sections focused on a theme or major, reside on the same residence hall floor with students with the same academic interests, or both. Learning community participation has grown from an initial cohort of 46 students in fall 1999 to 1,410 new beginning students in fall 2008.

SATS also coordinates the University's common reading program; a Twenty-First Century Scholars support site (one of 14 sites across the state that furnishes college preparation support for 6th-12th grade students from low-income and first-generation backgrounds); and Purdue Promise, a scholarship and support program for low-income and first-generation students from Indiana who enroll at the University. In the 2008-2009 academic year, SATS provided programs that served more than 25,000 students and families.

The decision to form the SATS department was not made in a vacuum; rather, it was the product of an ongoing examination of outcomes data by an array of faculty and staff who concluded that coordination yielded enhanced success rates for Purdue's newest students. In short, as the next section shows, SATS is living proof that the sum of the parts can indeed be greater than the individual parts themselves.

Research Design

The efficacy of the multilayered first-year experience program now coordinated by the SATS department at Purdue University is examined from a comprehensive approach involving both individual quasi-experimental program assessments and a simultaneous, complementary mixed-method design, exploring the overall impact of multiprogram participation. The following research questions drive program assessment:

- Does each individual program positively influence the students' academic outcomes as measured by retention rates, graduation rates, and grade point averages (GPAs)?
- Does the participation in multiple coordinated programs at the University provide a greater impact on students' experiences and academic outcomes when compared to the individual programs examined above?

For the quantitative individual program assessments, the participants' retention rates, graduation rates, and GPAs are compared to control groups of students of similar entry characteristics enrolled in the same academic schools and majors who voluntarily chose not to participate in the programs. For the multiprogram assessment, a logistic regression is used to examine both the relationships between single program participation and retention as well as multiprogram participation and retention. The major limitation to this research is self-selection bias. While the impact of student's pre-entry and demographic characteristics can be controlled for via design and analysis, the problem of self-selection bias by the participants is not examined.

Findings

The quantitative results for the individual programs indicate that program participation in the efforts now coordinated by SATS is positively related to academic success at Purdue. One-year retention rates for Boiler Gold Rush (BGR) participants are 8.03 percentage points higher (86.64% vs. 78.61%, $p < 0.0001$) than nonparticipants. Differences among females are even more dramatic, as female participants' one-year retention rates are 11.16 percentage points higher (86.90% vs. 75.74%, $p < 0.0001$) than female nonparticipants. Similarly, students who participated in the Summer Transition, Advising and Registration program have one-year retention rates that are 8.34 percentage points higher than nonparticipants (85.04% vs. 76.7%, $p < 0.0001$). Learning community participants are retained at a rate 7.02 percentage points higher than nonparticipants (91.48% vs. 84.46%, $p < 0.0001$). Differences among women and minority participants and nonparticipants are even larger than for the overall population (women 92.42% vs. 85.38%, $p < 0.0001$, minority 91.67% vs. 80.04%, $p < 0.01$).

The most recent logistic regression analysis examined the predictive capability of program participation, SAT scores, gender, ethnicity, high school rank, and college GPA on retention for 19,490 students over three academic years. The initial model only examined participation as a dichotomous variable, ignoring the impact of multiprogram participation. The results indicate that program participation is a significant predictor of retention even when pre-entry and demographic characteristics as well as college academic success are controlled for (Table 1). The second model examined the impact of multiprogram participation by further dividing participation into three reference groups (i.e., single program participation, multiprogram participation, nonparticipation). Results indicate that when multiprogram participation is entered into the model it is a significant predictor of retention, while single-program participation becomes nonsignificant, indicating the significant positive correlation between multi-program participation even when grades, academic preparation, and demographics are considered (Table 2).

Table 1

Logistic Regression Analysis of Overall Program Participation

Variable	β	S.E.	Wald	df	Sig	Exp(β)
Participants*	0.495	0.127	15.157	1	0.000	1.641
Sindex9	0.469	0.730	40.796	1	0.000	1.599
Gindex9	1.073	0.129	69.581	1	0.000	2.924
HSRANK	0.007	0.002	7.700	1	0.006	1.007
SATV	-0.002	0.001	6.056	1	0.014	0.998
SATM	0.001	0.001	0.827	1	0.363	1.001
Male**	0.159	0.092	2.973	1	0.085	1.173
Caucasian***	-2.689	15.713	0.029	1	0.864	0.068
Non-Caucasian***	-2.980	15.714	0.036	1	0.850	0.051
Constant	1.343	15.716	0.007	1	0.932	3.831

* Compared to nonparticipants, ** Compared to females, ***Compared to international.
Note. -2 Log Likelihood = 4393.34. Cox & Snell $R^2 = 0.069$. Nagelkerke $R^2 = 0.181$.

Table 2

Logistic Regression Analysis of Multiprogram Participation

Variable	β	S.E.	Wald	df	Sig	Exp(β)
Participants*	0.737	0.520	2.008	1	0.156	2.090
Two or more Programs Participants*	0.480	0.130	13.575	1	0.000	1.616
Sindex9	0.470	0.073	40.863	1	0.000	1.600
Gindex9	1.072	0.129	69.432	1	0.000	2.921
HSRANK	0.007	0.002	7.679	1	0.006	1.007
SATV	-0.002	0.001	6.050	1	0.014	0.998
SATM	0.001	0.001	0.813	1	0.367	1.001
Male**	0.160	0.092	2.993	1	0.084	1.173
International***	2.697	15.712	0.029	1	0.864	14.842
Non-Caucasian***	-0.291	0.126	5.317	1	0.021	0.748
Constant	-1.342	0.319	17.688	1	0.000	0.261

* Compared to nonparticipants, ** Compared to females, ***Compared to international.
Note. -2 Log Likelihood = 4393.34. Cox & Snell R^2 = 0.069. Nagelkerke R^2 = 0.181.

Implications and Future Directions

Given the evidence of the benefits of participation in multiple, intentionally coordinated first-year programs, the SATS department is making additional efforts to foster connections between the initiatives it conducts as well as other programs operated by Purdue's specific colleges and schools. The linkages with these unit-specific initiatives will forge additional meaningful connections—both intellectual and social—for students during their first and subsequent years of study at the University. The SATS department's efforts are being bolstered by Purdue University's recently approved strategic plan. Titled "New Synergies" and spanning the period between 2008-2014, the plan directly calls for "strong support services to increase success, retention, and graduation for students from all backgrounds" with an emphasis on forging connections between existing programs and addressing gaps between these programs as they are identified, As the research outcomes associated with this case show, SATS serves as a model of the kind of action called for by the institution's strategic plan.

Beyond Purdue, the outcomes of this project suggest that today's increasingly complex institutions of higher learning can serve their first-year students better by using data to intentionally coordinate their first-year experience efforts. In an increasingly sustainability-focused nation and world, this form of coordination can also help to eliminate duplication of effort, thereby, conserving resources while maximizing student learning, success, and other related outcomes.

Contributors

Andrew K. Koch
Director of Student Access, Transition and Success Programs
Purdue University
128 Memorial Mall Drive
Stewart Center G 77
Student Access, Transition and Success Programs
Purdue University
West Lafayette, Indiana 47907
Phone: 765-496-3618
E-mail: akkoch@purdue.edu

Brent M. Drake
Associate Director, Enrollment Management Analysis and Reporting
Purdue University
E-mail: bmdrake@purdue.edu

WALES

Faculty Advice Shops

University of Glamorgan

The Institution and Its Students

The University of Glamorgan, located in Pontypridd, Wales, UK, is a publicly controlled higher education institution. The total student population for 2006-2007 was 21,326, of which 86% were undergraduates and 14% postgraduate. Half (51%) were full-time, and 2,463 were international students. The male/female ratio was 49:51. Of the undergraduate population, 23% of full-time, and 54% of part-time students were age 25 or older. The ethnic demographics of the undergraduate population were Black 3%, **Asian** 6% (one third Chinese), White 83%, and other/undisclosed 7%. The percentage of students living in residential halls on campus was 5%.

Higher Education Statistics Agency (HESA) data show that 29.4% of the University's students are from low-participation neighborhoods, compared with 16.4% for Wales as a whole, and 14% across the UK (HESA, 2007a). HESA defines low-participation neighborhoods in the UK as "areas for which the participation rate is less than two thirds of the UK average rate" (HESA, 2007b). In addition, 41.4% of the University's students are from lower socioeconomic groups, compared with 29.0% for Wales and 29.3% across the UK (HESA, 2007a).

The Initiative

In 2006, the University of Glamorgan set up Faculty Advice Shops across the institution as one of its initiatives to address rising student drop-out rates and provide an interface for student/faculty interaction. Advice Shops are an innovative concept—not only providing frontline advice to students but also actively developing and implementing strategies to improve retention and progression based on the data they collect. Thus, the Advice Shops complement and integrate their roles and services with existing academic and administrative student support in the **faculty**. They also collaborate institutionally with Student Services and other corporate support departments. The major goals of the Advice Shops responding to student attrition include

- ◇ Identifying retention issues across the faculty in conjunction with faculty **staff**
- ◇ Implementing intervention processes to improve student retention within the faculty
- ◇ Identifying best practices across the University of Glamorgan and other institutions and to share examples where appropriate

This initiative arose from the success of a pilot Advice Shop, which was established in 2001 in the School of Humanities and Social Sciences (HASS). The school's senior management identified the need for an Advice Shop in response to two emerging developments: (a) the increasing number of students seeking academic help or advice on withdrawing, suspending, or transferring studies and (b) concern about the retention and progression patterns for first-year students. The role of the Advice Shop was to act as an information, advice, and referral service. The pilot was very successful and led to a lower attrition rate and significant revenue savings. Thus, Advice Shop was made a permanent feature of HASS.

In 2005, the University directorate made the decision to roll out this type of provision across the entire University, which was about to be reorganized into five faculties: (a) Advanced Technology; (b) Cardiff School of Creative and Cultural Industries; (c) Glamorgan Business School; (d) Health, Sport, and Science; and (e) Humanities and Social Sciences (Fitzgibbon & Carter, 2006). Accordingly, in September 2006, Advice Shops were opened in the four remaining faculties, extending the provision to all University of Glamorgan students and focusing on those students from widening-participation backgrounds and low-participation neighborhoods.

Each Advice Shop provides a full-time, drop-in service and appointment system for academic advice and pastoral support. Academic advice includes any aspect of the student's current or proposed course of study, including information and advice on withdrawal, transfer, or suspension of their studies. Pastoral support can include referral to corporate support providers within the University.

The Advice Shops are also actively involved in the identification and implementation of appropriate faculty-based interventions to support student retention. In addition to the common provision described above, a range of individual faculty-specific functions is designed to address retention issues. Examples include

- ◇ Electronic monitoring of attendance and proactive follow-up with first-year undergraduate students who have low or sporadic patterns of attendance
- ◇ Administering an undergraduate **summer revision** event for students with referrals in coursework and/or examination **assessments**
- ◇ Providing cross-faculty liaisons for disability and dyslexia support services
- ◇ Scheduling progress meetings for students identified as at risk of drop out or poor performance (e.g., late enrollees, repeating students, students failing or not submitting early assessment work)
- ◇ Becoming involved in the **induction** program for all first-year students and providing a central contact point for students enrolling late

Advice Shops are managed by a member of the **research-active academic staff** and supported by a range of administrative personnel, who participate in a number of faculty and University-wide strategic and operational committees.

Research Design

This study examines the provision of Advice Shops, which is an ongoing University-wide initiative. A multiphased approach has been adopted to identify student retention and achievement issues followed by analysis of the impact of the initiatives undertaken. The study follows an action research methodology (Cohen, Manion, & Morrison, 2007) and, as a result, is an iterative process that informs and reviews the work. The research questions include

- What factors contribute to making students at risk of early withdrawal?
- What interventions can be established to counteract these factors?
- What evidence is there of use and effectiveness of the interventions?
- What evidence is there of the impact on improving student retention?

As such, the research included (a) an examination of student retention rates, existing interventions, and known risk points or triggers; (b) the identification and selection of major interventions; (c) the implementation of identified interventions; and (d) gathering data to test the impact of the interventions.

Secondary research was carried out to address the first research question using findings from the established HASS Advice Shop, historical data from the University, and a literature review. To answer our second and third questions, we collected qualitative and quantitative data from primary sources, which involved (a) the development and implementation of a student record system to collect data on student interviews and contacts, (b) the development and distribution of online questionnaires to assess student satisfaction with Advice Shop provision, and (c) data collected from the attendance monitoring systems.

The final research question was addressed by collating Advice Shop data on student contact and usage and correlating common factors leading to dissatisfaction or early withdrawal from study.

Findings

What factors contribute to making students at risk of early withdrawal?

The retention literature identifies the main reasons for early withdrawal as poor social or academic integration (Beder, 1997; Crosling, Thomas, & Heagney, 2008; Tinto, 1993; Yorke & Longden, 2007), including transition to a higher education culture, lack of preparedness (Collins & Lim, 2002; Ozga & Sukhnandan, 1998), poor course choice (Yorke, 1999), financial and personal issues (such as ill health) or other supra-institutional factors (Archer, Hutchings, & Ross, 2003; Christie, Munro, & Fisher, 2004). As Figure 1 shows, many of the categories of withdrawal at Glamorgan matched those from the literature, with the notable exception of financial issues. This disparity is particularly striking given the demographic profile of the University and the number of students with significant commitments to part-time work.

Underlying the categories in Figure 1 were complex factors, which contribute to student withdrawal. These were manifested by low or nonattendance at time-tabled classes, nonsubmission or poor performance of early assessments, and difficulties with time management and the rigors of independent study. Many first-year undergraduate students struggled to adapt to the new learning environment, and this was exacerbated by trying to balance university with family, part-time work, and other commitments. Social integration was further affected by the numbers of commuting students who maintained their previous social circles from home.

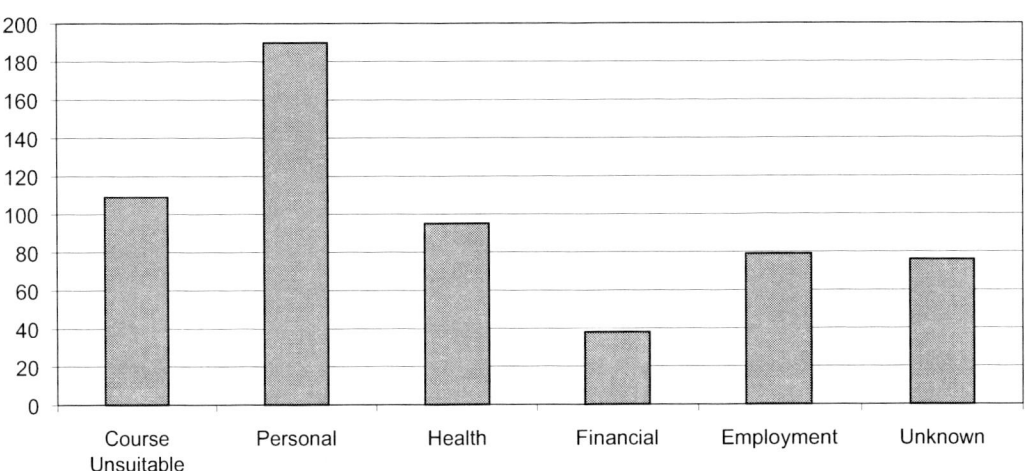

Figure 1. Reasons for in-year withdrawal and suspended studies, 2006-2007.

What interventions can be established to counteract these factors?

In response to the contributory factors identified above, we identified the following interventions, which were subsequently adopted by the Advice Shops:

- Providing a central point of contact within each faculty for any student query
- **Signposting** to other faculty and institutional support staff and services
- Following up with students who were expected to return but failed to re-enroll
- Advising students considering change of course of study or institution or early withdrawal
- Systematically monitoring attendance of first-year students and offering tutor referral for any other students
- Implementing a robust follow-up system for students with low or sporadic attendance patterns
- Targeting students with nonsubmission or late submission of assessments
- Holding progress meetings to encourage students to adopt successful study strategies
- Designing and implementing electronic self-assessment support tools to enable students to identify the extent of their social and academic orientation and integration
- Sponsoring events to encourage social integration

What evidence is there of the use and effectiveness of the interventions?

Following the opening of the Faculty Advice Shops, students immediately began to access the drop-in provision. Advice Shops were inundated with queries or requests for information, as well as more complex issues that required students to meet with an advisor. Over the period of October 2006 to June 2007, the volume of student usage from all types of inquiries including visits, e-mails, and telephone calls totalled 13,773. The majority of queries were managed within the Advice Shop, but where necessary, students were referred to the appropriate support staff or services and subsequently contacted to ensure a network of care. Advice Shop surveys of student opinion show that 69% were either satisfied or very satisfied with the service provided.

Where students failed to enroll when expected or suspended their studies, Advice Shop contact resulted in many of these students successfully returning to their studies. This contact provides help and advice on suitability of course and techniques for successful study. The effectiveness of the intervention was evidenced by the number of students subsequently returning to their studies (approximately 20%) or resuming after a period of suspension (more than 50%). The Advice Shop also supports students considering early withdrawal, suspension of studies, or transfer of course during the academic year. This ensures that students make an informed decision so that their choice is a supported and positive experience.

More than 2,000 first-year students were monitored for attendance, which proved to be one of the most effective methods for the early identification of students at risk of disengaging or poor performance. Students with low attendance were contacted and offered support to encourage them back into the classroom, rather than disciplining them for poor attendance. Of the many hundreds of students contacted, approximately two thirds resumed their studies, with the remaining students either seeking further support to resume or making informed decisions about their studies rather than drifting away. Student feedback on the attendance monitoring interventions was positive, with 81% stating the intervention had improved their attendance rates, and 92% of those who attended an advice interview stated that they found it helpful.

Interventions such as the follow-up of late or nonsubmission of coursework and progress meetings enabled Advice Shops to target support for students with academic issues. The learner support tools allowed students to self-identify their individual need for support. Approximately 1,500 students used these self-assessment tools, which was much greater than anticipated.

Social integration is encouraged by the organization of cultural events, informal get-togethers for specific student cohorts and end-of-term and end-of-year celebrations. Participation in these events is high, and students are very positive about the opportunity to make friends and integrate with their peers and tutors in social settings.

What evidence is there of the impact on improving student retention?

The Advice Shops have established a better understanding of students and the issues they face while studying in higher education. As recommended by the House of Commons Committee of Public Accounts (2008), the University now has reliable information concerning study crisis points, timing, and reasons for withdrawal, including the underlying complexities of the reasons why students leave early.

Early indications are that the Advice Shops are making a contribution to the overall improvement in student retention. Although it is too early to evaluate the extent to which such improvement is directly attributable to these interventions, the evidence shows that the Advice Shops have made a positive contribution to improving the student experience.

Implications and Future Directions

There was immediate acceptance and use of the Advice Shops by students, demonstrating the need for such provision. The intervention also improved our understanding of and ability to profile our students, whether they were persisters or early leavers. We discovered a number of issues that were critical to the success of this initiative. First, a cohesive team of Advice Shop managers is vital for professional support and parity of student provision. Yet, student retention can never be solely the responsibility of the Advice Shops. It is an issue that must be addressed by the whole institution. To secure institution-wide buy-in, support from senior-level management is crucial. Even with a competent management team and top-level support, time is needed for the Advice Shops to be accepted by faculty staff and to be integrated with existing support provision.

If we were to do anything differently in the future, it would be to manage our own and staff expectations better with regard to realistic and achievable milestones. We would also pay greater attention to the physical location of each Advice Shop in order to maximize accessibility, visibility, and efficiency.

We believe that this initiative can easily be adapted at other institutions but offer the following suggestions for a smooth adoption of the Advice Shop concept. First, educators should put systems in place to provide evidence of institutional issues and use this evidence to identify appropriate interventions. Next, it is important to remember that a micro approach to interventions can be an effective starting point. For example, educators should implement the scheme on a small scale before adopting it across the institution. While we often expect a dramatic transformation of student retention in the short term, it may be more realistic to aim for incremental gains. Finally, the Advice Shop concept should follow a supportive rather than a punitive approach, especially when monitoring student attendance. Supporting poor attenders back into the classroom rather than penalizing them has proved to be a highly successful strategy.

References

Archer, L., Hutchings, M., & Ross, A. (2003). *Higher education and social class: Issues of exclusion and inclusion*. Trowbridge: RoutledgeFalmer.

Beder, S. (1997). *Addressing the issues of social and academic integration for first year students*. Retrieved September 29, 2009, from http://ultibase.rmit.edu.au/Articles/dec97/beder1.htm

Christie, H., Munro, M., & Fisher, T. (2004). Leaving university early: Exploring the differences between continuing and non-continuing students. *Studies in Higher Education, 29*(5), 617-626.

Cohen, L., Manion, L., & Morrison K. (2007). *Research methods in education* (6th ed.). London: Routledge.

Collins, R., & Lim, H. (2002). *Great expectations*. York, UK: The Higher Education Academy. Retrieved September 29, 2009, from http://www.heacademy.ac.uk/assets/York/documents/resources/resourcedatabase/id479_great_expectations.pdf

Crosling G., Thomas, L., & Heagney, M. (2008). *Improving student retention in higher education*. Abingdon: Routledge.

Fitzgibbon, K., & Carter J. (2006, April). *Using one-stop shopping to aid student retention*. Paper presented at The First European First Year Experience Conference, Teesside, UK.

Higher Education Statistics Agency (HESA). (2007a). *Performance indicators in higher education in the UK 2005/06, Table T1a: Young full time first degree entrants*. Retrieved September 29, 2009, from http://www.hesa.ac.uk/index.php?option=com_content&task=view&id=586&Itemid=141

Higher Education Statistics Agency (HESA). (2007b). *PIs 2005/06: Definitions*. Retrieved September 29, 2009, from http://www.hesa.ac.uk/index.php/content/view/596/141/

House of Commons Committee of Public Accounts. (2008), *Staying the course: The retention of students on higher education courses*. Tenth Report of Session 2007-08, The Stationery Office Limited.

Ozga, J., & Sukhnandan, L. (1998). Undergraduate non-completion: Developing an explanatory model. *Higher Education Quarterly, 52*(3), 316-333.
Tinto, V. (1993). *Leaving college: Rethinking the causes and cures of student attrition* (2nd ed.). Chicago: University of Chicago Press.
Yorke, M. (1999). *Leaving early: Undergraduate non-completion in higher education*. London: Falmer.
Yorke, M., & Longden, B. (2007). *The first-year experience in higher education in the UK*. York: Higher Education Academy.

Contributors

Karen Fitzgibbon
Principal Lecturer, Advice Shop Manager
Faculty of Humanities and Social Sciences
University of Glamorgan
Pontypridd, CF37 1DL
Phone: 01443 482050
E-mail: kfitzgib@glam.ac.uk

Sue Stocking
Principal Lecturer, Advice Shop Manager
Faculty of Advanced Technology

Julie Prior
Senior Lecturer, Advice Shop Manager
Glamorgan Business School

Mary Ayre
Senior Lecturer, Advice Shop Manager
Faculty of Health, Sport, and Science

Conclusion

Diane Nutt and Denis Calderon

As we suggested in the introduction to this monograph, this collection should not be seen as providing a comprehensive view of the first-year experience on an international stage, but it does provide a taste of the varied and creative practices that have developed to support first-year students and enhance their learning experience across five continents. The 16 institutions represented here are diverse, but their stories represent a growing international commitment to providing an engaging environment for new students and a desire to enable first-years to achieve their potential.

We would like to close this monograph by identifying both from this collection and our own research some key areas where effective work is being done to enhance the first-year experience. It is exciting to see how far we have come over the last 30 years. In that time, the impetus to enhance the first-year experience has traveled around the world and now encompasses a variety of effective educational practices. These strategies generally relate to one or more of the following categories: (a) pre-entry work; (b) **induction** and transition support activities; (c) peer support and social connections within the higher education environment; (d) ongoing support efforts; (e) skills development; and, more recently, (e) holistic approaches. As institutions begin to explore how they might better serve commencing students, these strategies provide an ideal first step in developing an overarching plan for shaping the first-year experience at an individual institution.

1. *Pre-entry work.* While the majority of the examples in this collection relate to strategies for supporting students once they begin their higher education study, pre-entry work is an area of growing importance. Reaching out to students before they begin their studies is becoming recognized as a useful way to help them make the right choices and motivate them early on. A variety of work with feeder institutions, which include secondary schools and colleges, adult preparatory colleges, and community colleges in the USA, is taking place in a number of countries.

   Another example of pre-entry work, involves bringing accepted students to the institution before the fall academic term begins to participate in residential events, which frequently have an academic component. This type of activity—often called a bridge program in the USA—engages students before they begin their formal studies. Rushton's case study from the University of Ulster in Northern Ireland is one example. Some institutions are also exploring these programs as strategies for helping students make the transition from the first year of study to subsequent years.

2. *Induction and transition.* A number of case studies in this collection focused on induction and the transition into university, emphasizing the importance of the first few days or week of higher education. For example, Clark at the University of Auckland in New Zealand and Fisher-Stitt and Tam from York University, Canada, explored different examples of

peer-assisted transition and induction. Induction activities and events are highlighted in a variety of countries as providing a good basis for student success. For example, work at the University of Ulster has underscored the value of effective induction activities for supporting student retention (Cook, Rushton, McCormick, & Southall, 2005).

3. *Peer support*. Peer support has been introduced in a variety of ways in a number of contexts, some of which are included in this collection. As noted above, peers are often used in induction activities. The intervention program at Auckland University of Technology described by Carlson and Scarbrough included peer support provided by second- and third-year students to at-risk first-year students during induction and at other key transition points. The example from Kansai University in Japan shows students supporting and learning from each other in a peer-support class.

4. *Ongoing support efforts*. While helping students make the initial transition to higher education has been a concern at a number of institutions, other colleges and universities have explored ways to offer support to students throughout the entire first year of study. Ody and Carey describe the program at Manchester where senior students provide peer-assisted learning opportunities for newer students. The following case studies also present strategies designed to provide ongoing support: (a) the intervention program at Auckland University of Technology mentioned above, (b) the Retention Support Officers initiative at Teesside University in England, (c) the SciTec model from the University of Uppsala in Sweden, (d) the Faculty Advice Shops introduced at Glamorgan University in Wales, and (e) the Student Access, Transitions and Success Program at Purdue University in the USA. This collection also showcases the first-year seminar or similar first-year courses designed to support students during the first academic term or year. In this compilation, examples were provided by Ouakrime at Sidi Mohamad ben Habdallah University in Morocco and by Patton and Carpenter at Portland State University in the USA.

5. *Skills development*. A focus on skills development is key to strategies designed to help the underprepared student. As we suggested in the introduction and the overview of countries chapter, students' lack of preparation for higher education is a concern for many institutions. Several case studies focused on helping new students learn more effectively in the higher education environment. The case from Minho University in Portugal described a strategy for promoting students learning through instructional narratives. O'Shea at Newcastle University in Australia showed how transition to study workshops could be effective in helping students make the academic transition to university. At Wolverhampton in England, Purnell and Hughes described using new technologies (e.g., blogs and e-portfolios) to help students with their writing, a critical academic skill.

6. *Holistic approaches*. An institutional approach to the first-year experience. In many institutions, enhancing the first-year experience is now a concern, and as this collection shows, a wide range of strategies have been developed to support first-years more effectively. More recently, a number of institutions around the world have become more intentional in their attempts to improve the first-year experience for their students by developing a more holistic or institutional approach to the first year of higher education study. These strategies attempt to coordinate and integrate initiatives aimed at first-year students, rather than having such efforts happen piecemeal throughout the institution. The case provided by Botha and van Schalkwyk from Stellenbosch University in South Africa provides a glimpse of such a strategy in its early stages; however, this effort is already having an impact on student experience. Koch and Drake at Purdue University in the USA also describe strategies to coordinate and centralize efforts to support first-year students. Examples of other places with institutional strategies include: Teesside University in England (see Dodgson & Bolam, 2002; Harvey,

Drew, & Smith, 2006) and Queensland University of Technology in Australia (Kift, 2009; Nelson, Clarke, & Kift, 2009).

As the cases in this monograph demonstrate, those invested in first-year experience initiatives include professors and tutors (academic staff), those who work in support services, managers and university leaders, and researchers. Strategies have developed in different contexts in response to different national, local, and institutional conditions. Some strategies have focused on add-on support, others on classroom engagement, and still others on comprehensive, institution-wide initiatives. All of the cases should remind us that there are many people, in a range of roles, in our own institutions who care about students and want to enhance their chances of success. We hope that the case studies included here will provide the readers with ideas, encouragement, and evidence needed to develop and improve initiatives for first-year students on their own campuses.

References

Cook, A., Rushton, B. S., McCormick, S. M., & Southall, D. W. (2005). *Guidelines for the management of students in transition (The Star Project)*. Ulster: The University of Ulster.

Dodgson, R., & Bolam, H. (2002). *Student retention, support and widening participation in the North East of England* (Regional Widening Participation Project). Sunderland: Universities for the North East.

Harvey, L., Drew, S., & Smith, M. (2006). *The first-year experience: A review of literature for the Higher Education Academy*. Retrieved January 10, 2007, from http://www.heacademy.ac.uk/4887.html

Kift, S. (2009, May). Plenary presentation at the European First Year Experience 4th Annual Conference, Groningen, the Netherlands.

Nelson, K., Clarke, J., & Kift, S. (2009, May). *A holistic approach to the support and engagement of first year students: A retention strategy*. Paper presented at the European First Year Experience Conference, Groningen, the Netherlands.

Glossary of Terms

Term	Definition
60% course load	In Canada, a student must be registered for 60% of the required modules or courses at a particular level to be counted as full-time.
Accommodation/s	Student residences, residence halls
Adjunct course format	Additional, noncredit bearing courses that do not count toward the program or degree requirements. They may be attached to a specific course, or be available to all students at a particular level (e.g., all first-years). While these are usually taught by instructors, they could be student-led. Typically, focused on skill development.
Asian	A term used in many countries to define ethnicity of students whose families originate in the Asian subcontinent (i.e., India, Pakistan, Bangladesh, Nepal, Sri Lanka). However, in some countries this is also inclusive of East Asians, South East Asians, and Pacific Islanders, leading some to use more specific terms denoting country or region of origin.
Assessment(s)	An umbrella term referring to all types of student-generated work used to judge learning or progress (e.g., reports, essays, presentations, as well as sit-down examinations).
Assessment	Evaluation or research. In the USA, assessment refers to formal, systematic evaluation of outcomes related to a course, initiative, or program.
Associate bachelor's degree	Two-year higher education program, leading to an award, often in vocational or applied subjects. Similar to foundation degrees in England and Wales and to associate degrees awarded by community colleges in the USA.
Bologna Process	A process that aims to harmonize academic degree and quality assurance standards across the European Union. As part of this, degree programs would be no shorter than three years, a credit transfer system would be created, and mobility for students and faculty across Europe would be enhanced.
Course	Large bite of learning, sometimes called a program of study. The term may be used to differentiate disciplinary focus from credit value or degree focus. For example, in response to the question "What course are you on?", an appropriate answer would be English or Physics, rather than BSc or MA. Also see module. In some contexts, course may refer to a single module or unit within a larger program of study.
Faculty	Academic staff (professors). Also school or college. Where this refers to school or colleges within a larger institution, a faculty usually includes smaller departments under a broad disciplinary focus (e.g., faculty of social sciences).

Term	Definition
First-degree entrants	Students who are studying for bachelor's degrees; analogous to undergraduates in the USA
Induction	Welcome activities and organized events to assist students in making the transition to higher education, sometimes including academic induction. Also known as orientation (see below).
Lecturer	Academic member of staff or faculty. In some countries called professor
Maori	Indigenous people of New Zealand, who are now an ethnic minority and are generally under-represented in universities.
Mark	Grade or evaluatory classification of student work.
Module	Small bite of learning. Sometimes called a course or a short program. Several modules together make up a course or program of study. Modules can vary in size. For example, a module may be worth 20 credits toward an undergraduate degree program worth 360 credits.
Orientation	Also induction. Activities designed to help students with the transition to higher education. In many institutions around the world, this may include activities in the first week, sometimes called welcome week. However, both induction and orientation can occur before students arrive and, for a varied period of time, after they have entered the institution.
Pasifika	An ethnic minority in New Zealand. Pasifika people identify as Pacific (i.e., from the Pacific islands and their territories) via ancestry and descent
Registers	Records of attendance at classes. In the UK and Australasia, monitoring students' attendance at classes is a common strategy for identifying students at risk.
Research-active academic staff	Most staff in UK universities are expected to remain current in their academic discipline, produce original scholarship (i.e., publish in their discipline), and conduct some research. In some universities, however, academic staff may be either primarily lecturers or researchers. This term applies to staff who see research as a key priority in their role.
Signposting	Providing guidance to further help
Staff	Faculty, professors; also academic staff
Summer revision	Summer school. This is an opportunity to prepare for resit examinations, offered by some institutions in the UK to students who have failed a particular module. Resit examinations may be available in the autumn before the new academic year begins.
Timetabled	Included in the university or program schedule. This may signify formal recognition in some instances.

About the Editors

Denis Calderon recently retired as assistant director of learning and teaching development in the Centre for Learning and Quality Enhancement at Teesside University in northeast England. In this post, he had a key role in developing and implementing the University's Learning, Teaching, and Assessment Strategy and led teams of staff who had institution-wide responsibilities for student retention, e-learning, research-informed teaching, and work-based learning. From 2000 to 2009, he served as the University's liaison in its partnership with the National Resource Center for The First-Year Experience and Students in Transition at the University of South Carolina and in its role as cohost of the International Conference on The First-Year Experience. He was also closely involved in the establishment of the European First Year Experience Network. Calderon has undertaken consultancy work for a number of other UK universities on learning and teaching issues and has also undertaken work for both the UK's Higher Education Academy and the Quality Assurance Agency of England and Wales.

Diane Nutt is head of the Student Retention Team at Teesside University in northeast England. She is also a University teaching fellow. In her post at Teesside, she directs retention and first-year experience initiatives, working with staff at all levels to support students in their learning experience. In this role, she also oversees research projects on student experience particularly in relation to retention and first-year experience. She was instrumental in the development of the European First Year Experience Network, ran the first European First Year Experience Conference in 2006, and is chair of the Conference Series Organising Committee. She was herself a first-generation student who dropped out, only to return 10 years later to complete her degree. She also has a PhD in sociology and worked for several years as a lecturer in sociology. Currently as part of her role as head of the Student Retention Team, she provides consultancy support both inside Teesside University and beyond. This has included working with universities around Europe to explore strategies for supporting first-year students.